"HE INSCRIBED UPON A STONE"

Celebrating the Work of Jim Eisenbraun

SBL
SBL PRESS

S\B\L PRESS

Atlanta

Copyright © 2020 by Society of Biblical Literature

Contents

EISENBRAUNS HISTORY

JAMES EDWIN EISENBRAUN

July 13, 1948	Born in Lanchow, Gansu Province, China
1953–1959	Attended three-room school in Sagola, Michigan
1959–1964	Attended school in Minnesota, Iowa, and Illinois
June 1, 1969	Graduated from Wheaton College, Wheaton, Illinois BA in Archaeology with a minor in Philosophy
June 8, 1969	Married Merna Zimmerman
1972	MDiv, Grace Theological Seminary, Winona Lake, Indiana
1973	ThM, Grace Theological Seminary, Winona Lake, Indiana
1974	Ann Arbor, MI, Began as copyeditor of BASOR and BA
1974	MA, Near Eastern Studies, University of Michigan, Ann Arbor
July 1, 1975	Founded Eisenbrauns
1977	Daughter Johanna born
1978	Left University of Michigan, ABD
1978–1982	Professor of Hebrew and Old Testament, Grace Theological Seminary
1978	Published *Hebrew Verse Structure* by Michael Patrick O'Connor First original title for Eisenbrauns
1982–2017	Publisher, Eisenbrauns, Inc.
1987	Son Gabriel born
2017–2019	Consultant, Eisenbrauns imprint of Penn State University

CATALOG EXCERPTS

CATALOG 4, 1981

WE WOULD LIKE TO TAKE THIS OPPORTUNITY TO THANK YOU FOR YOUR support of and interest in our services. Many of you seem like friends even though we may have never met.

If you are interested in a bit of our history, please read on. While doing graduate work at the University of Michigan Ann Arbor, Jim tired of paying high prices for specialized works in his field of study—the ancient Near East. To save some money, we (Jim and Merna) started as a bookseller in 1975 with basically personal needs in mind. That took $25 and a trip to the courthouse. Soon we were ordering for friends and then publishing a typewritten list of a few titles for distribution. There seems to have been a need, judging from the response. All this was done from the living room of our mobile home; needless to say, it soon took over, and the baby slept amidst boxes and books.

Three years ago (1978) we moved to Winona Lake, where Jim has a full-time teaching position. The books soon outgrew our rec room, then our rented space in a shopping center, and we are now located in our new 4,000 sq.ft. building. If you are passing through and wish to visit us, you will find a somewhat "warehouse" atmosphere, but we are happy to accommodate over-the-counter sales as well as mail order.

We feel that, as well as studying and teaching, we can make a contribution to the field by supplying books at the lowest possible prices; we raise prices with regret and only when the publishers increase the list price. As volume increases, we have been pleased to increase discounts on publications from various publishers, as we are able to secure better discounts. We have also happily lowered prices on some imports due to the recent strengthening of the dollar against European currencies.

Throughout the growth, we have tried to keep the service personal; we regret having to resort to form letters on occasion, but felt that the tradeoff in overhead was necessary. However, if at any time you feel that we have not dealt fairly with you, please write to either of us personally; we may not be able to respond to you personally, but will bake every effort to be sure that the issue is resolved equitably.

Another factor that you as a customer should be aware of is that we operate on limited capital. While we attempt to have a good inventory of the highest volume titles, and particularly reference works, there are times when we do not have all the titles you want in stock at the time of your order. Our resupply is based on an ordering cycle dependent on our buying volume from each publisher; we order from the major publishers monthly, but others only once every two or three months, unless there is a special need. Occasionally your back-order may be caught at the wrong end of this cycle and may be delayed longer than we would wish. Of course, you may specify "no back-orders" or "do not ship after...."

Response to our type of bookselling has been gratifying; we wish we had the time to answer the letters of appreciation personally. If we have been able, in our way, to advance scholarship, we feel adequately rewarded.

Sincerely,
Jim and Merna Eisenbraun
August, 1981

P.S. Some of you have wondered about our logo; it was adapted froma gazelle on an Early Dynastic cylinder seal.

FROM CATALOG 7, 1986

... ANOTHER NOTE IS IN ORDER, IF FOR NO OTHER REASON THAN TO explain our purpose, and, iin relation to that, your expectations. Eisenbrauns began as an ordering service. Since that beginning, it has continued to be both an ordering service and a bookseller with a certain amount of inventory on hand (that inventory steadily continues to grow). But it is difficult to offer both substantial discounts andimmediate shipment of all the items you order! We are pleased to offer hard-to-acquire items, and to offer them at discount prices. In turn we ask for your understanding regarding an item that may be out of stock tempoarily.

Finally, come by and visit us! We are open Saturday mornings for those of you who may not be able to get away during the week. Thank you for the opportunity to be of service.

FROM CATALOG 15, 1994–1995

THE SCHOLAR'S SOURCE IS THE MAIL-ORDER BOOK SERVICE OF EISEN-brauns, Inc. From our modest beginnings as an informal service among colleagues, we have grown into an internationally recognized source for academic books. Scholar's Source 15 lists more than 2,500 of the academic titles availble from Eisenbrauns.

1995 marks our twentieth year of service to the academic community. Though we have grown much over the years, the heart of our service is still the same. We help scholars, students, and libraries purchase the books they need to facilitate their studies, and we offer those books at the best possible prices.

Eisenbrauns and the Scholar's Source are committed to discount prices and fast, friendly, personal service. Thanks again to the many scholars, students, and libraries who purchased books from us over the last twenty years.

FROM CATALOG 30, 2010–2011

EISENBRAUNS NOW HAS A FACEBOOK PAGE; WE URGE YOU TO BECOME A fan of Eisenbrauns. We have also begun a Twitter feed, featuring a deal of the day, with discounts up to 95% off. Follow us on Twitter to take advantage of these savings; these specials are posted on our Facebook page and sent via our RSS feeds, as well.

We welcome your feedback on how to assist you in acquiring the books, charts, and software you need. Please feel free to e-mail your questions or comments to us.

RETIREMENT ANNOUNCEMENT

I'M WRITING THIS NOTE AT THE END OF JULY, HAVING JUST RETURNED from the ISBL in Rome and the RAI in Paris and while preparing to attend the IOSOT in Aberdeen—and the latter will be my last official conference on behalf of Eisenbrauns/PSU Press. By the time you read this, all of this will be history: a new acquisitions editor will be in place to shepherd the Eisenbrauns imprint, and I will have entered "full retirement." Some of you have told me that my retirement is the end of an era; and it certainly is for me. It's been an incredible, mostly unplanned, and wonderful "ride" from the early days in graduate school in Ann Arbor until the present; along the way, we encountered some very difficult times and have had many deeply enjoyable times. Here are a few reflections on this bit of history.

Eisenbrauns began in a time and place that provided opportunities. It began as a book service, a way to provide difficult-to-access books for me and my fellow graduate students in Ann Arbor, at a time when mail-order bookselling was a novel idea. We soon added a pre-press component—the publishing industry was going through major changes as typesetting moved from hot lead typesetting on Linotype and similar devices and into what was called "cold type," a computer-drive photographic process. Entrée into this market now could be achieved with a $15,000 investment instead of hundreds of thousands of dollars. (This latter process lasted for about 15 years until the "desktop publishing" revolution came along, which substantially reduced the cost of investment in typesetting even further.) And, during the early years, as a poverty-stricken grad student, I was employed as a copyeditor and journal production manager by the late, great David Noel Freedman, who was perhaps the best editor of all time; from him I learned much of the skills and processes involved in publishing. Furthermore, Merna and I lived in Ann Arbor, which was the "short-run, sheet-fed offset printing capital of the world," meaning that it was the home of multiple printers that serviced the academic publishing world. We saw needs; and we said, essentially, "we can do that." Within 3 years, we were printing books under the Eisenbrans label, with a logo taken from an Early Dynastic Sumerian cylinder seal (it's an ibex, not a bird!) redrawn by Merna. All of this was developed without ever having a business plan; we learned as we went along. Why it succeeded for more than 4 decades where many others came and went is difficult to determine; we did have to learn to adapt to change, in technologies, in market, and many other areas. But one thing we always believed: we needed personal contact with our customers; and our customers were colleagues, not mere objects.

Forty-four years later, the company has ended as an independent entity. We have published in that time more than 650 books (as I like to say: many of them quite good!). And my prime spirit is one of gratitude. I'm grateful for the dozens of employees we've had through the years; as I often told them, I considered them colleagues in an important enterprise, and I was one the most privileged to meet the people who bought books from us. I'm grateful for the many authors we've had the honor to publish; you folks are the best! I'm grateful for the editorial boards who've helped me sort through what to publish and what to avoid; we couldn't have done this without you. I'm grateful for the presence of fellow student, polymath, and dear friend, Michael Patrick O'Connor, who served as a one-person corporate board on many occasions; perhaps the most brilliant person I've known, he left us much too soon, more than a decade ago. I'm grateful for the partnership and wisdom provided by my wife of 50 years, Merna Zimmerman Eisenbraun; she owned half of the stock in Eisenbrauns (hence the "s"; it's a plural of our last name, not a possessive!).

I'm grateful, too, that the imprint goes on, under the PSU Press aegis. The staff at PSU Press will see to the ongoing life of Eisenbrauns, and a new Acquisitions Editor will guide the ship. This is a good thing.

But for now, to all of you: thank you for the privilege of knowing you and serving you. It's been a profound honor.

EISENBRAUNS PUBLICATIONS
1980–2017

1980

Freedman, David Noel. *Pottery, Poetry, and Prophecy: Studies in Early Hebrew Poetry.*

O'Connor, Michael Patrick. *Hebrew Verse Structure.*

1981

Halpern, Baruch, and Jon D. Levenson, eds. *Traditions in Transformation: Turning Points in Biblical Faith; Festschrift Honoring Frank Moore Cross.*

Morrison, M. A., and David I. Owen, eds. *In Honor of Ernest R. Lacheman on His Seventy-Fifth Birthday, April 29, 1981.*

Young, Gordon D., ed. *Ugarit in Retrospect: Fifty Years of Ugarit and Ugaritic.*

1982

Ishida, Tomoo, ed. *Studies in the Period of David and Solomon and Other Essays: Papers Read at the International Symposium for Biblical Studies, Tokyo, 5–7 December, 1979.*

Owen, David I. *Neo-Sumerian Archival Texts Primarily from Nippur in the University Museum, the Oriental Institute and the Iraq Museum (NATN).*

1983

Bergstrasser, Gotthelf. *Introduction to the Semitic Languages: Text Specimens and Grammatical Sketches.*

Gerstenblith, Patty. *The Levant at the Beginning of the Middle Bronze Age.*

Hallo, William W. James C Moyer, and Leo G Perdue, eds. *Scripture in Context II: More Essays on the Comparative Method.*

Huffmon, H. B., F. A. Spina, and A. R. W. Green, eds. *The Quest for the Kingdom of God: Studies in Honor of George E. Mendenhall.*

Inch, Morris A. and Ronald F Youngblood, eds. *The Living and Active Word of God: Studies in Honor of Samuel J. Schultz.*

Meyers, Carol L., ed. *The Word of the Lord Shall Go Forth: Essays in Honor of David Noel Freedman in Celebration of His 60. Birthday.*

Millard, A. R., and D. J. Wiseman, eds. *Essays on the Patriarchal Narratives.*

Vasholz, Robert I. *Data for the Sigla of the BHS.*

1984

Beld, Scott G., William W. Hallo, and Piotr Michalowski. *The Tablets of Ebla: Concordance and Bibliography.*

Gage, Warren Austin. *The Gospel of Genesis: Studies in Protology and Eschatology.*

Perdue, Leo G., and Brian W. Kovacs, eds. *A Prophet to the Nations: Essays in Jeremiah Studies.*

1985

Haran, Menahem. *Temples and Temple-Service in Ancient Israel: an Inquiry into Biblical Cult Phenomena and the Historical Setting of the Priestly School.*

Kort, Ann, and Scott Morschauser, eds. *Biblical and Related Studies Presented to Samuel Iwry.*

1986

Ahlström, Gösta W. *Who Were the Israelites?*

Parker, S. Thomas. *Romans and Saracens: A History of the Arabian Frontier.*

Rendsburg, Gary A. *The Redaction of Genesis.*

1987

Barr, James. *Comparative Philology and the Text of the Old Testament: With Additions and Corrections.*

Borowski, Oded. *Agriculture in Iron Age Israel.*

Conrad, Edgar W., and Edward G. Newing, eds. *Perspectives on Language and Text: Essays and Poems in Honor of Francis I. Andersen's Sixtieth Birthday, July 28, 1985.*
Gordon, Cyrus H., Gary A. Rendsburg, and Nathan Winter, eds. *Eblaitica: Essays on the Ebla Archives and Eblaite Language.* Volume 1.
O'Connor, Michael Patrick, and David Noel Freedman, eds. *Backgrounds for the Bible.*
Owen, D. I., and M. A. Morrison, eds. *General Studies and Excavations at Nuzi 9/1.*
Pitard, Wayne T. *Ancient Damascus: A Historical Study of the Syrian City-State from Earliest Times until Its Fall to the Assyrians in 732 B.C.E.*

1988

Farrow, Douglas. *The Word of Truth and Disputes about Words.*
Fox, Michael V., ed. *Temple in Society.*
Golomb, David M., ed., with Susan T. Hollis. *Working with No Data: Semitic and Egyptian Studies Presented to Thomas O. Lambdin.*

1989

Bennett, W. J., and Jeffrey A. Blakely. *Tell el-Hesi: The Persian Period (Stratum V).* Edited by Kevin G. O'Connell, with Fred L. Horton Jr.
Farber, Walter, ed. *Schlaf, Kindchen, schlaf! Mesopotamische Baby-Beschwörungen und -Rituale.*
Gitin, Seymour, and William G. Dever, eds. *Recent Excavations in Israel: Studies in Iron Age Archaeology.*
Lacheman, Ernest R., and Maynard P. Maidman, eds. *Joint Expedition with the Iraq Museum at Nuzi VII.*
Longacre, Robert E. *Joseph: A Story of Divine Providence; A Text Theoretical and Textlinguistic Analysis of Genesis 37 and 39–48.*
Michalowski, Piotr, ed. *Lamentation over the Destruction of Sumer and Ur.*
Rast, Walter E., and R. Thomas Schaub. *Bâb edh-Dhrâʿ: Excavations at the Town Site (1975–1981).*
Tzaferis, Vassilios, ed. *Excavations at Capernaum, Volume 1: 1978–1982.*
Vardaman, E. Jerry, and Edwin M. Yamauchi, eds. *Chronos, Kairos, Christos: Nativity and Chronological Studies Presented to Jack Finegan.*

Waldman, Nahum M. *The Recent Study of Hebrew: A Survey of the Literature with Selected Bibliography.*
Waltke, Bruce K., and Michael Patrick O'Connor. *Introduction to Biblical Hebrew Syntax.*

1990

Bernal, Martin. *Cadmean Letters: The Transmission of the Alphabet to the Aegean and Further West before 1400 B.C.*
Cook, Edward M., ed. *Sopher Mahir: Northwest Semitic Studies Presented to Stanislav Segert.*
Firmage, Edwin B., Bernard G. Weiss, and John W. Welch, eds. *Religion and Law: Biblical-Judaic and Islamic Perspectives.*
Gammie, John G., and Leo G. Perdue, eds. *The Sage in Israel and the Ancient Near East.*
Gordon, Cyrus H., and Gary A. Rendsburg, eds. *Eblaitica: Essays on the Ebla Archives and Eblaite Language.* Volume 2.
Hemer, Colin J. *The Book of Acts in the Setting of Hellenistic History.* Edited by Conrad H. Gempf.
Meyers, Eric M., Carol L. Meyers, and James F. Strange, eds. *Excavations at the Ancient Synagogue of Gush Halav.*
Propp, William Henry, Baruch Halpern, and David Noel Freedman, eds. *The Hebrew Bible and Its Interpreters.*

1991

Dahlberg, Bruce T., and Kevin G. O'Connell, eds. *Tell el-Hesi IV: The Site and the Expedition.*
Fishbane, Michael, Emanuel Tov, and Weston W. Fields, eds. *Sha'arei Talmon: Studies in the Bible, Qumran, and Ancient Near East Presented to Shemaryahu Talmon.*
Longman, Tremper, III. *Fictional Akkadian Autobiography: A Generic and Comparative Study.*
Ollenburger, Ben C., Elmer A. Martens, and Gerhard F. Hasel, eds. *The Flowering of Old Testament Theology: A Reader in Twentieth-Century Old Testament Theology, 1930–1990.*
Stone, Elizabeth C., and David I. Owen. *Adoption in Old Babylonian Nippur and the Archive of Mannum-mešu-liṣṣur.*

Young, Gordon D., ed. *Mari in Retrospect: Fifty Years of Mari and Mari Studies.*

1992

Black, David Alan, ed. *Scribes and Scripture: New Testament Essays in Honor of J. Harold Greenlee.*

Bodine, Walter R., ed. *Linguistics and Biblical Hebrew.*

Freedman, David Noel, A. Dean Forbes, and Francis I. Andersen, eds. *Studies in Hebrew and Aramaic Orthography.*

Gal, Zvi. *Lower Galilee during the Iron Age.*

Gonen, Rivka. *Burial Patterns and Cultural Diversity in Late Bronze Age Canaan.*

Gordon, Cyrus H., and Gary A. Rendsburg, eds. *Eblaitica: Essays on the Ebla Archives and Eblaite Language.* Volume 3.

House, Paul R., ed. *Beyond Form Criticism: Essays in Old Testament Literary Criticism.*

Leonard, Albert, ed. *AASOR 50: The Jordan Valley Survey, 1953 Some Unpublished Soundings Conducted by James Mellaart.*

Meyers, Eric M., Ehud Netzer, and Carol L. Meyers. *Sepphoris.*

Steinkeller, Piotr, and J. N. Postgate. *Third-Millennium Legal and Administrative Texts in the Iraq Museum, Baghdad.*

Weinfeld, Moshe. *Deuteronomy and the Deuteronomic School.*

1993

Christensen, Duane L., ed. *A Song of Power and the Power of Song: Essays on the Book of Deuteronomy.*

Eakins, J. Kenneth. *Tell el-Hesi, the Muslim Cemetery in Fields V and VI/IX (Stratum II).* Edited by John R. Spencer, with Kevin G. O'Connell.

George, A. R., ed. *House Most High: The Temples of Ancient Mesopotamia.*

Hess, Richard S. *Amarna Personal Names.*

Lacheman, Ernest R., Martha A. Morrison, and David I. Owen. *The Eastern Archives of Nuzi and Excavations at Nuzi 9/2.*

Malone, Joseph L. *Tiberian Hebrew Phonology.*

McConville, J. G. *Judgment and Promise: An Interpretation of the Book of Jeremiah.*

Snell, Daniel C. *Twice-Told Proverbs and the Composition of the Book of Proverbs.*

1994

Berlin, Adele. *Poetics and Interpretation of Biblical Narrative.*
Franke, Chris. *Isaiah 46, 47, and 48: A New Literary-Critical Reading.*
Gopher, Avi. *Arrowheads of the Neolithic Levant: A Seriation Analysis.*
Handy, Lowell K. *Among the Host of Heaven: The Syro-Palestinian Pantheon as Bureaucracy.*
Hess, Richard S., and David Toshio Tsumura, eds. *I Studied Inscriptions from Before the Flood: Ancient Near Eastern, Literary, and Linguistic Approaches to Genesis 1–11.*
Hopfe, Lewis M., ed. *Uncovering Ancient Stones: Essays in Memory of H. Neil Richardson.*
Millard, A. R., James K. Hoffmeier, and David W. Baker, eds. *Faith, Tradition, and History: Old Testament Historiography in Its Near Eastern Context.*

1995

Bottéro, Jean. *Textes culinaires mésopotamiens: Mesopotamian culinary texts.*
Gordon, Robert P., ed. *"The Place Is Too Small for Us": The Israelite Prophets In Recent Scholarship.*
Kelm, George L., and Amihai Mazar. *Timnah: A Biblical City in the Sorek Valley.*
Owen, David I., ed. *General Studies and Excavations at Nuzi 9/3.*
Wright, David P., David Noel Freedman, and Avi Hurvitz, eds. *Pomegranates and Golden Bells: Studies in Biblical, Jewish, and Near Eastern Ritual, Law, and Literature in Honor of Jacob Milgrom.*
Zevit, Ziony Zevit, Seymour Gitin, and Michael Sokoloff, eds. *Solving Riddles and Untying Knots: Biblical, Epigraphic, and Semitic Studies in Honor of Jonas C. Greenfield.*

1996

Bartelt, Andrew H. *The Book around Immanuel: Style and Structure in Isaiah 2–12.*

Carter, Charles E., and Carol L. Meyers, eds. *Community, Identity, and Ideology: Social Science Approaches to the Hebrew Bible.*

Coleson, Joseph E., and Victor H. Matthews, eds. *Go to the Land I Will Show You: Studies in Honor of Dwight W. Young.*

Cooper, Jerrold S., and Glenn M. Schwartz, eds. *The Study of the Ancient Near East in the Twenty-First Century: The William Foxwell Albright Centennial Conference.*

Fox, Michael V., Victor Avigdor Hurowitz, Avi M. Hurvitz, Michael L. Klein, Baruch J. Schwartz, and Nili Shupak, eds. *Texts, Temples, and Traditions: A Tribute to Menahem Haran.*

Lambert, Wilfred G. *Babylonian Wisdom Literature.*

Miller, Douglas B., and R. Mark Shipp. *An Akkadian Handbook: Paradigms, Helps, Glossary, Logograms, and Sign List.*

Putnam, Frederic Clarke. *A Cumulative Index to the Grammar and Syntax of Biblical Hebrew.*

Regt, L. J. de, J. de Waard, and Jan P. Fokkelman, eds. *Literary Structure and Rhetorical Strategies in the Hebrew Bible.*

Sanders, Donald H., ed. *Nemrud Dagi: The Hierothesion of Antiochus I of Commagene; Results of the American Excavations Directed by Theresa B. Goell.* 2 vols.

Schmidt, Brian B. *Israel's Beneficent Dead: Ancestor Cult and Necromancy in Ancient Israelite Religion and Tradition.*

Seger, Joe D., ed. *Retrieving the Past: Essays on Archaeological Research and Methodology in Honor of Gus W. Van Beek.*

1997

Afsaruddin, Asma, and A.H. Mathias Zahniser, eds. *Humanism, Culture, and Language in the Near East: Studies in Honor of Georg Krotkoff.*

Cogan, Mordechai Cogan, Barry L. Eichler, and Jeffrey H. Tigay, eds. *Tehillah le-Moshe: Biblical and Judaic Studies in Honor of Moshe Greenberg.*

Frerichs, Ernest S., and Leonard H. Lesko, eds. *Exodus: The Egyptian Evidence.*

Howard, David M., Jr. *The Structure of Psalms 93–100.*
Kaye, Alan S., and Peter T. Daniels, eds. *Phonologies of Asia and Africa.* 2 vols.
Keel, Othmar. *The Symbolism of the Biblical World: Ancient Near Eastern Iconography and the Book of Psalms.*
Lundbom, Jack R. *Jeremiah: A Study in Ancient Hebrew Rhetoric.*
Van Dam, Cornelis. *The Urim and Thummim: A Means of Revelation in Ancient Israel.*
Van Seters, John. *In Search of History: Historiography in the Ancient World and the Origins of Biblical History.*
Waard, Jan de. *A Handbook on Isaiah.*
Westenholz, Joan Goodnick. *Legends of the Kings of Akkade: The Texts.*

1998

Bennett, Patrick R. *Comparative Semitic Linguistics: A Manual.*
Horowitz, Wayne. *Mesopotamian Cosmic Geography.*
Izre'el, Shlomo, Itamar Singer, and Ran Zadok, eds. *Past Links: Studies in the Languages and Cultures of the Ancient Near East Dedicated to Professor Anson F. Rainey.*
Payne Smith, J., ed. *A Compendious Syriac Dictionary: Founded upon the Thesaurus Syriacus of R. Payne Smith.*
Rubin, Uri, and David J. Wasserstein, eds. *Dhimmis and Others: Jews and Christians and the World of Classical Islam.*

1999

Arazi, Albert, Joseph Sadan, and David J. Wasserstein, eds. *Compilation and Creation in Adab and Luga: Studies in Memory of Naphtali Kinberg (1948–1997).*
Chazan, Robert, William W. Hallo, and Lawrence H. Schiffman, eds. *Ki Baruch hu: Ancient Near Eastern, Biblical, and Judaic Studies in Honor of Baruch A. Levine.*
Dick, Michael B., ed. *Born in Heaven, Made on Earth: The Making of the Cult Image in the Ancient Near East.*
Freedman, David Noel. *Psalm 119: The Exaltation of Torah.*
Lambert, Wilfred G., Alan R. Millard, and Miguel Civil. *Atra-ḫasīs: The Babylonian Story of the Flood.*

Long, V. Philips, ed. *Israel's Past in Present Research: Essays on Ancient Isra-elite Historiography.*

Meyers, Eric M., ed. *Galilee through the Centuries: Confluence of Cultures.*

Miller, Cynthia L., ed. *The Verbless Clause in Biblical Hebrew: Linguistic Approaches.*

Moorey, P. R. S. *Ancient Mesopotamian Materials and Industries: The Archaeological Evidence.*

Russell, John Malcolm. *The Writing on the Wall: Studies in the Architectural Context of Late Assyrian Palace Inscriptions.*

Sparks, Kenton L. *Ethnicity and Identity in Ancient Israel: Prolegomena to the Study of Ethnic Sentiments and Their Expression in the Hebrew Bible.*

2000

Ben-Hayyim, Ze'ev, and Abraham Tal. *A Grammar of Samaritan Hebrew: Based on the Recitation of the Law in Comparison with the Tiberian and Other Jewish Traditions.*

Callender, Dexter E., Jr. *Adam in Myth and History: Ancient Israelite Perspectives on the Primal Human.*

Fleming, Daniel E. *Time at Emar: The Cultic Calendar and the Rituals from the Diviner's Archive.*

George, A. R., and I. L. Finkel, eds. *Wisdom, Gods and Literature: Studies in Assyriology in Honour of W. G. Lambert.*

Grayson, A. Kirk. *Assyrian and Babylonian Chronicles.*

Knoppers, Gary N., and J. Gordon McConville, eds. *Reconsidering Israel and Judah: Recent Studies on the Deuteronomistic History.*

Kutsko, John F. *Between Heaven and Earth: Divine Presence and Absence in the Book of Ezekiel.*

Penchansky, David, and Paul L. Redditt, eds. *Shall Not the Judge of All the Earth Do What Is Right? Studies on the Nature of God in Tribute to James L. Crenshaw.*

Stager, Lawrence E., Joseph A. Greene, and Michael D. Coogan, eds. *The Archaeology of Jordan and Beyond: Essays in Honor of James A. Sauer.*

Walsh, Carey Ellen. *The Fruit of the Vine: Viticulture in Ancient Israel.*

2001

Izreʾel, Shlomo. *Adapa and the South Wind: Language has the Power of Life and Death.*

LaRocca-Pitts, Elizabeth C. *Of Wood and Stone: The Significance of Israelite Cultic Items in the Bible and Its Early Interpreters.*

Nöldeke, Theodor. *Compendious Syriac Grammar.*

Pentiuc, Eugen J. *West Semitic Vocabulary in the Akkadian Texts from Emar.*

Schloen, J. David. *The House of the Father as Fact and Symbol: Patrimonialism in Ugarit and the Ancient Near East.*

Wright, David P. *Ritual in Narrative: The Dynamics of Feasting, Mourning, and Retaliation Rites in the Ugaritic Tale of Aqhat.*

2002

Abusch, Tzvi. *Riches Hidden in Secret Places: Ancient Near Eastern Studies in Memory of Thorkild Jacobsen.*

Bierling, Marilyn R., ed. and trans. *The Phoenicians in Spain: An Archaeological Review of the Eighth–Sixth Centuries B.C.E.; A Collection of Articles Translated from Spanish.*

Briant, Pierre. *From Cyrus to Alexander: A History of the Persian Empire.*

Cohen, Susan L. *Canaanites, Chronologies, and Connections: The Relationship of Middle Bronze IIA Canaan to Middle Kingdom Egypt.*

Ehrenberg, Erica Ehrenberg, ed. *Leaving No Stones Unturned: Essays on the Ancient Near East and Egypt in Honor of Donald P. Hansen.*

Gittlen, Barry M., ed. *Sacred Time, Sacred Place: Archaeology and the Religion of Israel.*

Gordon, Cyrus H., and Gary A. Rendsburg, eds. *Eblaitica: Essays on the Ebla Archives and Eblaite Language.* Volume 4.

Grosby, Steven. *Biblical ideas of Nationality: Ancient and Modern.*

Izreʾel, Shlomo, ed. *Semitic Linguistics: The State of the Art at the Turn of the Twenty-First Century.*

Porten, Bezalel, and Jerome A. Lund. *Aramaic Documents from Egypt: A Key-Word-In-Context Concordance.*

Roberts, J. J. M. *The Bible and the Ancient Near East: Collected Essays.*

Sharon, Diane M. *Patterns of Destiny: Narrative Structures of Foundation and Doom in the Hebrew Bible.*

Yener, K. Aslihan, and Harry A. Hoffner Jr., with Simrit Dhesi, eds. *Recent Developments in Hittite Archaeology and History: Papers in Memory of Hans G. Güterbock.*

2003

Beckman, Gary, Beckman, Richard Beal, and Gregory McMahon, eds. *Hittite Studies in Honor of Harry A. Hoffner Jr.: On the Occasion of His 65th Birthday.*

Cross, Frank Moore. *Leaves from an Epigrapher's Notebook: Collected Papers in Hebrew and West Semitic Palaeography and Epigraphy.*

Dever, William G., and Seymour Gitin, eds. *Symbiosis, Symbolism, and the Power of the Past: Canaan, Ancient Israel, and Their Neighbors from the Late Bronze Age through Roman Palaestina.*

Futato, Mark D. *Beginning Biblical Hebrew.*

Green, Alberto R. W. *The Storm-God in the Ancient Near East.*

Heimpel, Wolfgang. *Letters to the King of Mari: A New Translation, with Historical Introduction, Notes, and Commentary.*

Lipschits, Oded, and Joseph Blenkinsopp, eds. *Judah and the Judeans in the Neo-Babylonian Period.*

Magness, Jodi. *The Archaeology of the Early Islamic Settlement in Palestine.*

Moran, William L. *Amarna Studies: Collected Writings.* Edited by John Huehnergard and Shlomo Izre'el.

Talmon, Rafael. *Eighth-Century Iraqi Grammar: A Critical Exploration of Pre-Halilian Arabic Linguistics.*

Rast, Walter E., and R. Thomas Schaub. *Bāb edh-Dhrāʿ: Excavations at the Town Site (1975–1981).*

Richard, Suzanne. *Near Eastern Archaeology: A Reader.*

Strawn, Brent A., and Nancy R. Bowen, eds. *A God So Near: Essays on Old Testament Theology in Honor of Patrick D. Miller.*

Waard, Jan de. *A Handbook on Jeremiah.*

2004

Batto, Bernard F., and Kathryn L. Roberts, eds. *David and Zion: Biblical Studies in Honor of J. J. M. Roberts.*

Chapman, Cynthia R. *The Gendered Language of Warfare in the Israelite-Assyrian Encounter.*

Cohen, Chaim, Avi M. Hurvitz, and Shalom M. Paul, eds. *Sefer Moshe: The Moshe Weinfeld Jubilee Volume; Studies in the Bible and the Ancient Near East, Qumran, and Post-biblical Judaism.*
Fried, Lisbeth S. *The Priest and the Great King: Temple-Palace Relations in the Persian Empire.*
Friedman, Richard Elliott, and William H. C. Propp, eds. *Le-David Maskil: A Birthday Tribute for David Noel Freedman.*
Garr, W. Randall. *Dialect Geography of Syria-Palestine, 1000–586 B.C.E.*
Heller, Roy L. *Narrative Structure and Discourse Constellations: An Analysis of Clause Function in Biblical Hebrew Prose.*
Kessler, Martin, ed. *Reading the Book of Jeremiah: A Search for Coherence.*
Lessing, R. Reed. *Interpreting Discontinuity: Isaiah's Tyre Oracle.*
Ollenburger, Ben C., ed. *Old Testament Theology: Flowering and Future.*
Olmo Lete, Gregorio del. *Canaanite Religion: According to the Liturgical Texts of Ugarit.*
Stone, Elizabeth C., and Paul Zimansky. *The Anatomy of a Mesopotamian City: Survey and Soundings at Mashkan-Shapir.*
Tetley, M. Christine. *The Reconstructed Chronology of the Divided Kingdom.*

2005

Cohen, Eran. *The Modal System of Old Babylonian.*
Dunn, James D. G., and Scot McKnight., eds. *The Historical Jesus in Recent Research.*
Gane, Roy E. *Cult and Character: Purification Offerings, Day of Atonement, and Theodicy.*
Huehnergard, John. *A Grammar of Akkadian.* 2nd ed.
Huehnergard, John. *Key to a Grammar of Akkadian.* 2nd ed.
Kalimi, Isaac. *The Reshaping of Ancient Israelite History in Chronicles.*
Kofoed, Jens Bruun. *Text and History: Historiography and the Study of the Biblical Text.*
Langer, Ruth, and Steven Fine, eds. *Liturgy in the Life of the Synagogue: Studies in the History of Jewish Prayer.*
Lipschits, Oded. *The Fall and Rise of Jerusalem: Judah under Babylonian Rule.*
Master, Daniel M., ed. *Dothan: Remains from the Tell (1953–1964).*

Na'aman, Nadav. Ancient *Israel and Its Neighbors: Interaction and Counteraction; Collected Essays.*
Na'aman, Nadav. *Canaan in the Second Millennium B.C.E.: Collected Essays.*
Rubin, Aaron D. *Studies in Semitic Grammaticalization.*
Strong, John T., and Steven S. Tuell, eds. *Constituting the Community: Studies on the Polity of Ancient Israel in Honor of S. Dean McBride, Jr.*
Troxel, Ronald L., Kelvin G. Friebel, and Dennis R. Magary, eds. *Seeking Out the Wisdom of the Ancients: Essays Offered to Honor Michael V. Fox on the Occasion of His Sixty-Fifth Birthday.*
Tsumura, David Toshio. *Creation and Destruction: A Reappraisal of the Chaoskampf Theory in the Old Testament.*

2006

Amit, Yairah, Ehud Ben Zvi, Israel Finkelstein, and Oded Lipschits, eds. *Essays on Ancient Israel in Its Near Eastern Context: A Tribute to Nadav Na'aman.*
Fassberg, Steven E., and Avi Hurvitz, eds. *Biblical Hebrew in Its Northwest Semitic Setting: Typological and Historical Perspectives.*
Gitin, Seymour, J. Edward Wright, and J. P. Dessel, eds. *Confronting the Past: Archaeological and Historical Essays on ancient israel in Honor of William G. Dever.*
Japhet, Sara. *From the Rivers of Babylon to the Highlands of Judah: Collected Studies on the Restoration Period.*
Kogan, Leonid E., Natalia Koslova, Sergey Loesov, and Serguei Tishchenko, eds. *Babel und Bibel 2: Memoriae Igor M. Diakonoff.*
Lipschits, Oded, and Manfred Oeming, eds. *Judah and the Judeans in the Persian Period.*
Maeir, Aren M., and Pierre de Miroschedji, eds. *"I Will Speak the Riddles of Ancient Times": Archaeological and Historical Studies in Honor of Amihai Mazar on the Occasion of His Sixtieth Birthday.*
McKenzie, Steven L. *The Chronicler's Use of the Deuteronomistic History.*
Na'aman, Nadav. *Ancient Israel's History and Historiography: The First Temple Period.*
Shields, Martin A. *The End of Wisdom: A Reappraisal of the Historical and Canonical Function of Ecclesiastes.*
Ska, Jean-Louis. *Introduction to Reading the Pentateuch.*

Van Seters, John. *The Edited Bible: The Curious History of the "Editor" in Biblical Criticism.*

Vogt, Peter T. *Deuteronomic Theology and the Significance of Torah: A Reappraisal.*

Whitney, K. William, Jr. *Two Strange Beasts: Leviathan and Behemoth in Second Temple and Early Rabbinic Judaism.*

Yon, Marguerite. *The City of Ugarit at Tell Ras Shamra.*

2007

Heinz, Marlies, and Marian H. Feldman, eds. *Representations of Political Power: Case Histories from Times of Change and Dissolving Order in the Ancient Near East.*

Kaye, Alan S., ed. *Morphologies of Asia and Africa.*

Klingbeil, Gerald A. *Bridging the Gap: Ritual and Ritual Texts in the Bible.*

Knohl, Israel. *The Sanctuary of Silence: The Priestly Torah and the Holiness School.*

Knoppers, Gary N., and Bernard M. Levinson, eds. *The Pentateuch as Torah: New Models for Understanding Its Promulgation and Acceptance.*

Kogan, Leonid E., Natalia Koslova, Sergey Loesov, and Serguei Tishchenko, eds. *Babel und Bibel 3.*

Kravitz, Kathryn F., and Diane M. Sharon, eds. *Bringing the Hidden to Light: The Process of Interpretation; Studies in Honor of Stephen A. Geller.*

Lambert, W. G. *Babylonian Oracle Questions.*

Lipschits, Oded, Gary N. Knoppers, and Rainer Albertz, eds. *Judah and the Judeans in the Fourth Century B.C.E.*

Livingstone, Alasdair. *Mystical and Mythological Explanatory Works of Assyrian and Babylonian Scholars.*

Malena, Sarah, and David Miano, eds. *Milk and Honey: Essays on Ancient Israel and the Bible in Appreciation of the Judaic Studies Program at the University of California, San Diego.*

Mettinger, Tryggve N. D. *The Eden Narrative: A Literary and Religio-historical Study of Genesis 2–3.*

Parpola, Simo. *Letters from Assyrian Scholars to the Kings Esarhaddon and Ashurbanipal.* 2 vols.

Wilcke, Claus. *Early Ancient Near Eastern Law: A History of Its Beginnings; The Early Dynastic and Sargonic Periods.* 2nd ed.

Younger, K. Lawson, Jr., ed. *Ugarit at Seventy-Five.*

2008

Arav, Rami, ed. *Cities through the Looking Glass: Essays on the History and Archaeology of Biblical Urbanism.*

Burke, Aaron A. *"Walled Up to Heaven": The Evolution of Middle Bronze Age Fortification Strategies in the Levant.*

Cohen, Chaim, Victor Avigdor Hurowitz, Avi M. Hurvitz, Yochanan Muffs, Baruch J. Schwartz, and Jeffrey H. Tigay, eds. *Birkat Shalom: Studies in the Bible, Ancient Near Eastern Literature, and Postbiblical Judaism Presented to Shalom M. Paul on the Occasion of His Seventieth Birthday.*

Dolansky, Shawna. *Now You See It, Now You Don't: Biblical Perspectives on the Relationship between Magic and Religion.*

Hess, Richard S., Gerald A. Klingbeil, and Paul J. Ray Jr., eds. *Critical Issues in Early Israelite History.*

Hess, Richard S., and Elmer A. Martens, eds. *War in the Bible and Terrorism in the Twenty-First Century.*

Hoffner, Harry A., Jr., and H. Craig Melchert. *A Grammar of the Hittite Language.*

Huehnergard, John. *Ugaritic Vocabulary in Syllabic Transcription.*

Johnson, Barbara l. *Ashkelon 2: Imported Pottery of the Roman and Late Roman Periods.*

Korchin, Paul D. *Markedness in Canaanite and Hebrew Verbs.*

Levtow, Nathaniel B. *Images of Others: Iconic Politics in Ancient Israel.*

Nissinen, Martti, and Risto Uro, eds. *Sacred Marriages: The Divine-Human Sexual Metaphor from Sumer to Early Christianity.*

Qimron, Elisha. *The Hebrew of the Dead Sea Scrolls.*

Ross, Micah, ed. *From the Banks of the Euphrates: Studies in Honor of Alice Louise Slotsky.*

Rothe, Russell D., William K. Miller, and George (Rip) Rapp. *Pharaonic Inscriptions from the Southern Eastern Desert of Egypt.*

Stager, Lawrence E., J. David Schloen, and Daniel M. Master, eds. *Ashkelon 1: Introduction and Overview (1985–2006).*

Tappy, Ron E., and P. Kyle McCarter Jr., eds. *Literate Culture and Tenth-Century Canaan: The Tel Zayit Abecedary in Context.*

2009

Boda, Mark J. *A Severe Mercy: Sin and Its Remedy in the Old Testament.*

Bordreuil, Pierre, and Dennis Pardee. *A Manual of Ugaritic.*

Cohen, Yoram. *The Scribes and Scholars of the City of Emar in the Late Bronze Age.*

Dessel, J. P. *Lahav I: Pottery and Politics; The Halif Terrace Site 101 and Egypt in the Fourth Millennium B.C.E.*

Eidevall, Göran. *Prophecy and Propaganda: Images of Enemies in the Book of Isaiah.*

Fox, Nili Sacher, David A. Glatt-Gilad, and Michael J. Williams, eds. *Mishneh Todah: Studies in Deuteronomy and Its Cultural Environment in Honor of Jeffrey H. Tigay.*

Hess, Richard S. *Studies in the Personal Names of Genesis 1–11.*

Holsinger-Friesen, Thomas. *Irenaeus and Genesis: A Study of Competition in Early Christian Hermeneutics.*

Isaak, Jon, ed. *The Old Testament in the Life of God's People: Essays in Honor of Elmer A. Martens.*

Japhet, Sara. *The Ideology of the Book of Chronicles and Its Place in Biblical Thought.*

Kalimi, Isaac. *The Retelling of Chronicles in Jewish Tradition and Literature: A Historical Journey.*

Kim, Yoo-Ki. *The Function of the Tautological Infinitive in Classical Biblical Hebrew.*

Knoppers, Gary N., and Kenneth A. Ristau, eds. *Community Identity in Judean Historiography: Biblical and Comparative Perspectives.*

Lohr, Joel N. *Chosen and Unchosen: Conceptions of Election in the Pentateuch and Jewish-Christian Interpretation.*

Meyers, Eric M., and Carol L. Meyers. *Excavations at Ancient Nabratein: Synagogue and Environs.*

Olofsson, Staffan. *Translation Technique and theological Exegesis: Collected Essays on the Septuagint Version.*

Porter, Barbara Nevling, ed. *What Is a God? Anthropomorphic and Nonanthropomorphic Aspects of Deity in Ancient Mesopotamia.*

Schloen, J. David, ed. *Exploring the Longue Durée: Essays in Honor of Lawrence E. Stager.*

Smith, Mark S. *The Origins and Development of the Waw-Consecutive: Northwest Semitic Evidence from Ugarit to Qumran.*

Sokoloff, Michael. *A Syriac Lexicon: A Translation from the Latin; Correction, Expansion, and Update of C. Brockelmann's Lexicon Syriacum.* Copublished with Gorgias Press.

Van Seters, John. *The Biblical Saga of King David.*

Wells, Bruce, and Rachel Magdalene, eds. *Law from the Tigris to the Tiber: The Writings of Raymond Westbrook.*

Wolde, Ellen van. *Reframing Biblical Studies: When Language and Text Meet Culture, Cognition, and Context.*

2010

Blau, Joshua. *Phonology and Morphology of Biblical Hebrew: An Introduction.*

Earl, Douglas S. *Reading Joshua as Christian Scripture.*

Gosline, Sheldon Lee. *Writing Late Egyptian Hieratic: A Beginner's Primer.*

Hardin, James Walker. *Lahav II: Households and the Use of Domestic Space at Iron II Tell Halif; An Archaeology of Destruction.*

Jindo, Job Y. *Biblical Metaphor Reconsidered: A Cognitive Approach to Poetic Prophecy in Jeremiah 1–24.*

Kazen, Thomas. *Issues of Impurity in Early Judaism.*

Kazen, Thomas. *Jesus and Purity Halakhah: Was Jesus Indifferent to impurity?* 2nd ed.

Kogan, Leonid E., Natalia Koslova, Sergey Loesov, and Serguei Tishchenko, eds. *Proceedings of the 53rd Rencontre Assyriologique Internationale.* Vol. 1: *Language in the Ancient Near East* (2 parts); Vol. 2: *City Administration in the Ancient Near East.*

Kouwenberg, N. J. C. *The Akkadian Verb and Its Semitic Background.*

Lapinkivi, Pirjo. *The Neo-Assyrian Myth of Ištar's Descent and Resurrection: Introduction, Cuneiform Text, and Transliteration with a Translation, Glossary, and Extensive Commentary.*

Liss, Hanna, and Manfred Oeming, eds. *Literary Construction of Identity in the Ancient World: Proceedings of the Conference Literary Fiction and the Construction of Identity in Ancient Literatures: Options and Limits of Modern Literary Approach.*

Meyers, Eric M., and Paul V. M. Flesher, eds. *Aramaic in Postbiblical Judaism and Early Christianity: Papers from the 2004 National Endowment for the Humanities Summer Seminar at Duke University.*

Moshavi, Adina. *Word Order in the Biblical Hebrew Finite Clause: A Syntactic and Pragmatic Analysis of Preposing.*

Noll, K. L. Noll, and Brooks Schramm, eds. *Raising Up a Faithful Exegete: Essays in Honor of Richard D. Nelson.*

Rönnegård, Per. *Threads and Images: The Use of Scripture in Apophthegmata Patrum.*

Schmid, Konrad. *Genesis and the Moses Story: Israel's Dual Origins in the Hebrew Bible.*

Talmon, Shemaryahu. *Text and Canon of the Hebrew Bible: Collected Studies.*

Weiss, Zeev, Oded Irshai, Jodi Magness, and Seth Schwartz, eds. *Follow the Wise: Studies in Jewish History and Culture in Honor of Lee I. Levine.*

2011

Albrektson, Bertil. *History and the Gods: An Essay on the Idea of Historical Events as Divine Manifestations in the Ancient Near East and in Israel.*

Álvarez-Mon, Javier, and Mark B. Garrison, eds. *Elam and Persia.*

Anderson, John E. *Jacob and the Divine Trickster: A Theology of Deception and YHWH's Fidelity to the Ancestral Promise in the Jacob Cycle.*

Bembry, Jason. *Yahweh's Coming of Age.*

Ben Zvi, Ehud, and Diana Edelman, eds. *What Was Authoritative for Chronicles?*

Cantrell, Deborah O'Daniel. *The Horsemen of Israel: Horses and Chariotry in Monarchic Israel (Ninth–Eighth Centuries B.C.E.).*

Chesson, Meredith S., ed. *Daily Life, Materiality, and Complexity in Early Urban Communities of the Southern Levant: Papers in Honor of Walter E. Rast and R. Thomas Schaub.*

Conklin, Blane. *Oath Formulas in Biblical Hebrew.*

Eidevall, Göran, and Blaženka Scheuer, eds. *Enigmas and Images: Studies in Honor of Tryggve N. D. Mettinger.*

Finkelstein, Israel, and Nadav Na'aman, eds. *The Fire Signals of Lachish: Studies in the Archaeology and History of Israel in the Late Bronze Age, Iron Age, and Persian Period in Honor of David Ussishkin.*

Frankel, David. *The Land of Canaan and the Destiny of Israel: Theologies of Territory in the Hebrew Bible.*

Galor, Katharina, and Gideon Avni, eds. *Unearthing Jerusalem: 150 years of Archaeological Research in the Holy City.*

Gross, Andrew D., ed. *In Pursuit of Meaning: Collected Studies of Baruch A. Levine*. 2 vols.

Grossman, Jonathan. *Esther: The Outer Narrative and the Hidden Reading*.

Heimpel, Wolfgang, and Gabriella Frantz-Szabó, eds. *Strings and Threads: A Celebration of the Work of Anne Draffkorn Kilmer*.

Leichty, Erle. *The Royal Inscriptions of Esarhaddon, King of Assyria (680–669 BC)*.

Levinson, Bernard M. *The Right Chorale: Studies in Biblical Law and Interpretation*.

Lipschits, Oded, Gary N. Knoppers, and Manfred Oeming, eds. *Judah and the Judeans in the Achaemenid Period: Negotiating Identity in an International Context*.

Lipschits, Oded, and David S. Vanderhooft. *The Yehud Stamp Impressions: A Corpus of Inscribed Impressions from the Persian and Hellenistic Periods in Judah*.

Marchesi, Gianni, and Nicolo Marchetti. *Royal Statuary of Early Dynastic Mesopotamia*.

Michalowski, Piotr. *The Correspondence of the Kings of Ur: An Epistolary History of an Ancient Mesopotamian Kingdom*.

Moon, Joshua N. *Jeremiah's New Covenant: An Augustinian Reading*.

Morgenstern, Matthew. *Studies in Jewish Babylonian Aramaic: Based upon Early Eastern Manuscripts*.

Pongratz-Leisten, Beate, ed. *Reconsidering the Concept of Revolutionary Monotheism*.

Roitto, Rikard. *Behaving as a Christ-Believer: A Cognitive Perspective on Identity and Behavior Norms in Ephesians*.

Roskop, Angela. *The Wilderness Itineraries: Genre, Geography, and the Growth of Torah*.

Schlimm, Matthew Richard. *From Fratricide to Forgiveness: The Language and Ethics of Anger in Genesis*.

Stager, Lawrence E., Daniel M. Master, and J. David Schloen, eds. *Ashkelon 3: The Seventh Century B.C.*

Steiner, Richard C. *Early Northwest Semitic Serpent Spells in the Pyramid Texts*.

Tadmor, Hayim, and Shigeo Yamada. *The Royal Inscriptions of Tiglath-Pileser III (744–727 BC) and Shalmaneser V (726–722 BC), Kings of Assyria*.

Walton, John H. *Genesis 1 as Ancient Cosmology*.

Way, Kenneth C. *Donkeys in the Biblical World: Ceremony and Symbol.*

2012

Albertz, Rainer, and Rudiger Schmitt. *Family and Household Religion in Ancient Israel and the Levant.*

Andersen, Francis I., and A. Dean Forbes. *Biblical Hebrew Grammar Visualized.*

Barthélemy, Dominique. *Studies in the Text of the Old Testament: An Introduction to the Hebrew Old Testament Text Project.*

Burer, Michael H. *Divine Sabbath Work.*

Cohen, Eran. *Conditional Structures in Mesopotamian Old Babylonian.*

Cook, John A. *Time and the Biblical Hebrew Verb: The Expression of Tense, Aspect, and Modality in Biblical Hebrew.*

Faust, Avraham. *The Archaeology of Israelite Society in Iron Age II.*

Grayson, A. Kirk, and Jamie Novotny. *The Royal Inscriptions of Sennacherib, King of Assyria (704–681 BC).* Part 1.

Hawkins, Ralph K. *The Iron Age I Structure on Mt. Ebal: Excavation and Interpretation.*

Hwang, Jerry. *The Rhetoric of Remembrance: An Investigation of the "Fathers" in Deuteronomy.*

Kalimi, Isaac, ed. *Jewish Bible Theology: Perspectives and Case Studies.*

Kalimi, Isaac, ed. *New Perspectives on Ezra-Nehemiah: History and Historiography, Text, Literature, and Interpretation.*

Kogan, Leonid E., N. Koslova, S. Loesov, and S. Tishchenko, eds. *Babel und Bibel 6.*

Meyers, Eric M., and Carol Meyers, eds. *Archaeology, Bible, Politics, and the Media: Proceedings of the Duke University Conference, April 23–24, 2009.*

Mierse, William E. *Temples and Sanctuaries from the Early Iron Age Levant: Recovery after Collapse.*

Miller-Naudé, Cynthia L., and Ziony Zevit, eds. *Diachrony in Biblical Hebrew.*

Parker, Bradley J., and Catherine P. Foster, eds. *New Perspectives on Household Archaeology.*

Porter, Anne M., and Glenn M. Schwartz, eds. *Sacred Killing: The Archaeology of Sacrifice in the Ancient Near East.*

Press, Michael D. *Ashkelon 4: The Iron Age Figurines of Ashkelon and Philistia.*

Saysell, Csilla. *"According to the Law": Reading Ezra 9–10 as Christian Scripture.*

Schloen, J. David, and Sandra R. Schloen. *OCHRE: An Online Cultural and Historical Research Environment.*

Schmitz, Philip C. *The Phoenician Diaspora: Epigraphic and Historical Studies.*

Strahan, Joshua Marshall. *The Limits of a Text: Luke 23:34a as a Case Study in Theological Interpretation.*

Wasserman, Nathan. *Most Probably: Epistemic Modality in Old Babylonian.*

Wilhelm, Gernot, ed. *Organization, Representation, and Symbols of Power in the Ancient Near East: Proceedings of the 54th Rencontre Assyriologique Internationale at Wuerzburg, 20–25 July 2008.*

Zetterholm, Magnus, and Samuel Byrskog, eds. *The Making of Christianity: Conflicts, Contacts, and Constructions; Essays in Honor of Bengt Holmberg.*

2013

Azzoni, Annalisa. *The Private Lives of Women in Persian Egypt.*

Batto, Bernard F. *In the Beginning: Essays on Creation Motifs in the Ancient Near East and the Bible.*

Boda, Mark J., Tremper Longman III, and Cristian G. Rata, eds. *The Words of the Wise Are Like Goads: Engaging Qoheleth in the 21st Century.*

Boda, Mark J., and Lissa M. Wray Beal, eds. *Prophets, Prophecy, and Ancient Israelite Historiography.*

Borowski, Oded. *Lahav III: The Iron Age II Cemetery at Tell Halif (Site 72).*

Cohen, Ohad. *The Verbal Tense System in Late Biblical Hebrew Prose.*

Cooley, Jeffrey L. *Poetic Astronomy in the Ancient Near East: The Reflexes of Celestial Science in Ancient Mesopotamian, Ugaritic, and Israelite Narrative.*

Davidovich, Tal. *Esther, Queen of the Jews: The Status and Position of Esther in the Old Testament.*

Dell, Katharine J. *Interpreting Ecclesiastes: Readers Old and New.*

DeRouchie, Jason S., Jason Gile, and Kenneth J. Turner, eds. *For Our Good Always: Studies on the Message and Influence of Deuteronomy in Honor of Daniel I. Block.*

Evans, Paul S., and Tyler F. Williams, eds. *Chronicling the Chronicler: The Book of Chronicles and Early Second Temple Historiography.*

Feliu, L., J. Llop, A. Millet Alba, and J. Sanmartin, eds. *Time and History in the Ancient Near East: Proceedings of the 56th Rencontre Assyriologique Internationale at Barcelona 26–30 July 2010.*

Finkelstein, Israel, David Ussishkin, and Eric H. Cline, eds. *Megiddo V: The 2004–2008 Seasons.* 3 vols.

Garfinkle, Steven J., and Manuel Molina, eds. *From the 21st Century B.C. to the 21st Century A.D.: Proceedings of the International Conference on Neo-Sumerian Studies Held in Madrid 22–24 July 2010.*

Gordon, Robert P., and Hans M. Barstad, eds. *"Thus Speaks Ishtar of Arbela": Prophecy in Israel, Assyria, and Egypt in the Neo-Assyrian Period.*

Heim, Knut Martin. *Poetic Imagination in Proverbs: Variant Repetitions and the Nature of Poetry.*

Holm, Tawny L. *Of Courtiers and Kings: The Biblical Daniel Narratives and Ancient Story-Collections.*

Holmstedt, Robert D., and Aaron Schade, eds. *Linguistic Studies in Phoenician: In Memory of J. Brian Peckham.*

Keener, Hubert James. *A Canonical Exegesis of the Eighth Psalm: YHWH's Maintenance of the Created Order through Divine Intervention.*

Lambert, W. G. *Babylonian Creation Myths.*

Levinson, Bernard M. *A More Perfect Torah: At the Intersection of Philology and Hermeneutics in Deuteronomy and the Temple Scroll.*

Lowery, Daniel DeWitt. *Toward a Poetics of Genesis 1–11: Reading Genesis 4:17–22 in Its Near Eastern Context.*

Mann, Steven T. *Run, David, Run! An Investigation of the Theological Speech Acts of David's Departure and Return (2 Samuel 14–20).*

Mathews, Joshua G. *Melchizedek's Alternative Priestly Order: A Compositional Analysis of Genesis 14:18–20 and Its Echoes throughout the Tanak.*

Mettinger, Tryggve N. D. *No Graven Image? Israelite Aniconism in its Ancient Near Eastern Context.*

Mettinger, Tryggve N. D. *The Riddle of Resurrection: "Dying and Rising Gods" in the Ancient Near East.*

Meyers, Eric M., and Carol L. Meyers, eds. *The Pottery from Ancient Sepphoris.*

Norin, Stig. *Personennamen und Religion im alten Israel: Untersucht mit besonderer Berücksichtigung der Namen auf El und Ba'al.*

Schwáb, Zoltán S. *Toward an Interpretation of the Book of Proverbs: Selfishness and Secularity Reconsidered.*

Scurlock, JoAnn, and Richard H. Beal, eds. *Creation and Chaos: A Reconsideration of Hermann Gunkel's Chaoskampf Hypothesis.*

Seger, Joe D. *Gezer VII: The Middle Bronze and Later Fortifications in Fields II, IV, and VIII.*

Stern, Ephraim. *The Material Culture of the Northern Sea Peoples in Israel.*

Talmon, Shemaryahu. *Literary Motifs and Patterns in the Hebrew Bible: Collected Studies.*

Tarrer, Seth B. *Reading with the Faithful: Interpretation of True and False Prophecy in the Book of Jeremiah from Ancient to Modern.*

Van Seters, John. *The Yahwist: A Historian of Israelite Origins.*

Vanderhooft, David S., and Abraham Winitzer, eds. *Literature as Politics, Politics as Literature: Essays on the Ancient Near East in Honor of Peter Machinist.*

Wazana, Nili. *All the Boundaries of the Land: The Promised Land in Biblical Thought in Light of the Ancient Near East.*

2014

Ackerman, Susan, Charles E. Carter, and Beth Alpert Nakhai, eds. *Celebrate Her for the Fruit of Her Hands: Essays in Honor of Carol L. Meyers.*

Aitken, James K. *No Stone Unturned: Greek Inscriptions and Septuagint Vocabulary.*

Albertz, Rainer, Beth Alpert Nakhai, Saul M. Olyan, and Rüdiger Schmitt, eds. *Family and household Religion: Toward a Synthesis of Old Testament Studies, Archaeology, Epigraphy, and Cultural Studies.*

Altmann, Peter, and Janling Fu, eds. *Feasting in the Archaeology and Texts of the Bible and the Ancient Near East.*

Arnold, Bill T., Nancy L. Erickson, and John H. Walton, eds. *Windows to the Ancient World of the Hebrew Bible: Essays in Honor of Samuel Greengus.*

Babcock, Bryan C. *Sacred Ritual: A Study of the West Semitic Ritual Calendars in Leviticus 23 and the Akkadian Text Emar 446.*

Barker, Joel. *From the Depths of Despair to the Promise of Presence: A Rhetorical Reading of the Book of Joel.*

Beckman, Gary M. *The Babilili-Ritual from Hattusa: (CTH 718).*

Bekins, Peter. *Transitivity and Object Marking in Biblical Hebrew: An Investigation of the Object Preposition ʾet.*

Dallaire, Hélène. *The Syntax of Volitives in Biblical Hebrew and Amarna Canaanite Prose.*

Dever, William G. *Excavations at the Early Bronze IV Sites of Jebel Qaʿaqir and Beʿer Resisim.*

Edelman, Diana V., and Ehud Ben Zvi, eds. *Memory and the City in Ancient Israel.*

Elayi, J., and A.G. Elayi. *A Monetary and Political History of the Phoenician City of Byblos in the Fifth and Fourth Centuries B.C.E.*

Farber, Walter. *Lamaštu: An Edition of the Canonical Series of Lamaštu Incantations and Rituals and Related Texts from the Second and First Millennia B.C.*

Fincke, Jeanette C., ed. *Divination in the Ancient Near East: A Workshop on Divination Conducted during the 54th Rencontre Assyriologique Internationale, Würzburg, 2008.*

Garroway, Kristine Henriksen. *Children in the Ancient Near Eastern Household.*

Gilmour, Garth. *Gezer VI: The Objects from Phases I and II (1964–1974).*

Grayson, A. Kirk, and Jamie Novotny. *The Royal Inscriptions of Sennacherib, King of Assyria (704–681 BC).* Part 2.

Hackett, Jo Ann, and Walter E. Aufrecht, eds. *"An Eye for Form": Epigraphic Essays in Honor of Frank Moore Cross.*

Hoffmeier, James K., ed. *Tell el-Borg I: Excavations in North Sinai; The "Dwelling of the Lion" on the Ways of Horus.*

Kitz, Anne Marie. *Cursed Are You! The Phenomenology of Cursing in Cuneiform and Hebrew Texts.*

Knafl, Anne Katherine. *Forming God: Divine Anthropomorphism in the Pentateuch.*

Kogan, Leonid E., ed. *Babel und Bibel 7.*

Koskie, Steven Joe, Jr. *Reading the Way to Heaven: A Wesleyan Theological Hermeneutic of Scripture.*

Koslova, Natalia, E. Vizirova, and Gabor Zólyomi, eds. *Babel und Bibel 8: Studies in Sumerian Language and Literature; Festschrift Joachim Krecher.*

Kozuh, Michael. *The Sacrificial Economy: Assessors, Contractors, and Thieves in the Management of Sacrificial Sheep at the Eanna Temple of Uruk (ca. 625–520 B.C.)*.

Marti, Lionel, ed. *La famille dans le Proche-Orient ancien: Réalités, symbolismes, et images; Proceedings of the 55th Rencontre Assyriologique Internationale at Paris, 6–9 July 2009*.

Miller, Douglas B., and R. Mark Shipp. *An Akkadian Handbook: Helps, Paradigms, Glossary, Logograms, and Sign List*.

Peckham, J. Brian. *Phoenicia: Episodes and Anecdotes from the Ancient Mediterranean*.

Petter, Thomas D. *The Land between the Two Rivers: Early Israelite Identities in Central Transjordan*.

Porten, Bezalel, and Ada Yardeni. *Textbook of Aramaic Ostraca from Idumea*. Volume 1.

Samet, Nili. *The Lamentation over the Destruction of Ur*.

Spencer, John R., Robert A. Mullins and Aaron J. Brody, eds. *Material Culture Matters: Essays on the Archaeology of the Southern Levant in Honor of Seymour Gitin*.

Viberg, Ake. *Prophets in Action: An Analysis of Prophetic Symbolic Acts in the Old Testament*.

Weeks, Stuart. *The Making of Many Books: Printed Works on Ecclesiastes 1523–1875*.

Wikander, Ola. *Drought, Death, and Sun in Ugarit and Ancient Israel: A Philological and Comparative Study*.

2015

Abusch, Tzvi. *Male and Female in the Epic of Gilgamesh: Encounters, Literary History, and Interpretation*.

Archi, Alfonso, ed. *Tradition and Innovation in the Ancient Near East: Proceedings of the 57th Rencontre Assyriologique Internationale at Rome 4–8 July 2011*.

Bautch, Richard J., and Gary N. Knoppers, eds. *Covenant in the Persian period: From Genesis to Chronicles*.

Beit-Arieh, Itzhaq, and Liora Freud. *Tel Malḥata: A Central City in the Biblical Negev*. 2 vols.

Borrelli, Noemi. *The Umma Messenger Texts from the Harvard Semitic Museum and the Yale Babylonian Collection*.

Campbell, Dennis R. M. *Mood and Modality in Hurrian.*

Carroll R., M. Daniel, and J. Blair Wilgus, eds. *Wrestling with the Violence of God: Soundings in the Old Testament.*

Chan, Michael J., and Brent A. Strawn, eds. *What Kind of God? Collected Essays of Terence E. Fretheim.*

Cole, Dan P. Lahav V: *The Iron, Persian, and Hellenistic Occupations within the Walls at Tell Halif; Excavations in Field II, 1977–1980.*

Collins, Steven, Carroll M. Kobs, and Michael C. Luddeni. *The Tall al-Hammam Excavations.*

Cook, Edward M. *Dictionary of Qumran Aramaic.*

Davies, Gwyn, and Jodi Magness. *The 2003–2007 Excavations in the Late Roman Fort at Yotvata.*

Fales, Frederick M., and J. N. Postgate. *Imperial Administrative Records, Part 2: Provincial and Military Administration.*

Fox, R. Michael. *A Message from the Great King: Reading Malachi in Light of Ancient Persian Royal Messenger Texts from the Time of Xerxes.*

Hicks, Jonathan. *Trinity, Economy, and Scripture: Recovering Didymus the Blind.*

Hillers, Delbert R. *Poets before Homer: Collected Essays on Ancient Literature.* Edited by F. W. Dobbs-Allsopp.

Hoag, Gary G. *Wealth in Ancient Ephesus and the First Letter to Timothy: Fresh Insights from Ephesiaca by Xenophon of Ephesus.*

Huster, Yaakov. *Ashkelon 5: The Land behind Ashkelon.*

Jacobs, Paul F. *Lahav IV: The Figurines of Tell Halif.*

Janeway, Brian. *Sea Peoples of the Northern Levant? Aegean-Style Pottery from Early Iron Age Tell Tayinat.*

Jenks, R. Gregory. *Paul and His Mortality: Imitating Christ in the Face of Death.*

Keel, Othmar, and Silvia Schroer. *Creation: Biblical Theologies in the Context of the Ancient Near East.*

Kratz, Reinhard G. *The Prophets of Israel.*

McDowell, Catherine L. *The Image of God in the Garden of Eden: The Creation of Humankind in Genesis 2:5-3:24 in Light of the* mīs pî pīt pî *and* wpt-r *Rituals of Mesopotamia and Ancient Egypt.*

Mettinger, Tryggve N. D. *Reports From a Scholar's Life: Select Papers on the Hebrew Bible.* Edited by Andrew Knapp.

Miller, Marvin Lloyd, Ehud Ben Zvi, and Gary N. Knoppers, eds. *The Economy of Ancient Judah in Its Historical Context.*

Nielsen, John P. *Personal Names in Early Neo-Babylonian Legal and Administrative tablets, 747–626 B.C.E.*

Oeming, Manfred, and Konrad Schmid. *Job's Journey: Stations of Suffering.*

Ooi, Vincent K. H. *Scripture and Its Readers: Readings of Israel's Story in Nehemiah 9, Ezekiel 20, and Acts 7.*

Saner, Andrea D. *Too Much to Grasp: Exodus 3:13–15 and the Reality of God.*

Sasson, Jack M. *From the Mari Archives: An Anthology of Old Babylonian Letters.*

Schmid, Konrad. *Is There theology in the Hebrew Bible?*

Steinberg, Julius, and Timothy J. Stone, eds. *The Shape of the Writings.*

Tov, Emanuel. *The Text-Critical Use of the Septuagint in Biblical Research.* 3rd ed.

Troxel, Ronald L. *Joel: Scope, Genre(S), and Meaning.*

Werman, Cana, ed. *From Author to Copyist: Essays on the Composition, Redaction, and Transmission of the Hebrew Bible in Honor of Zipi Talshir.*

Widmer, Michael. *Standing in the Breach: An Old Testament Theology and Spirituality of Intercessory Prayer.*

Wilson, Ian Douglas, and Diana V. Edelman, eds. *History, Memory, Hebrew Scriptures: A Festschrift for Ehud Ben Zvi.*

Yona, S., E. L. Greenstein, M. I. Gruber, P. Machinist, and S. M. Paul, eds. *Marbeh Ḥokmah: Studies in the Bible and the Ancient Near East in Loving Memory of Victor Avigdor Hurowitz.*

2016

Assis, Elie. *Identity in Conflict: The Struggle between Esau and Jacob, Edom and Israel.*

Baranowski, Krzysztof J. *The Verb in the Amarna Letters from Canaan.*

Barker, Kit. *Imprecation as Divine Discourse: Speech Act Theory, Dual Authorship, and Theological Interpretation.*

Bartoloni, Gilda, and Maria Giovanna Biga, eds. *Not Only History: Proceedings of the Conference in Honor of Mario Liverani Held in Sapienza-Università di Roma, Dipartimento di scienze dell'Antichità, 20–21 April 2009.*

Benz, Brendon C. *The Land before the Kingdom of Israel: A History of the Southern Levant and the People Who Populated It.*

Bosworth, David A. *Infant Weeping in Akkadian, Hebrew, and Greek Literature.*

Bunimovitz, Shlomo, and Zvi Lederman. *Tel Beth-Shemesh: A Border Community in Judah; Renewed Excavations 1990–2000; The Iron Age.*

Butts, Aaron Michael. *Language Change in the Wake of Empire: Syriac in Its Greco-Roman Context.*

Eggleston, Chad L. *See and Read All These Words: The Concept of the Written in the Book of Jeremiah.*

Fincke, Jeanette C., ed. *Divination as Science: A Workshop Conducted during the 60th Rencontre Assyriologique Internationale, Warsaw, 2014.*

Garr, W. Randall, and Steven E. Fassberg, eds. *A Handbook of Biblical Hebrew.* 2 vols.

Haydon, Ronald. *Seventy Sevens Are Decreed: A Canonical Approach to Daniel 9:24–27.*

Hayes, Elizabeth R., and Karolien Vermeulen, eds. *Doubling and Duplicating in the Book of Genesis: Literary and Stylistic Approaches to the Text.*

Herzog, Ze'ev, and Lily Singer-Avitz. *Beer-Sheba III: The Early Iron IIA Enclosed Settlement and the Late Iron IIA–Iron IIB Cities.* 3 vols.

Hoffmeier, James K., Alan R. Millard, and Gary A. Rendsburg, eds. *Did I Not Bring Israel Out of Egypt? Biblical, Archaeological, and Egyptological Perspectives on the Exodus Narratives.*

Holmstedt, Robert D. *The Relative Clause in Biblical Hebrew.*

Johnson, Dru. *Knowledge by Ritual: A Biblical Prolegomenon to Sacramental Theology.*

Kogan, Leonid E., ed. *Babel und Bibel 9: Proceedings of the 6th Biennial Meeting of the International Association for Comparative Semitics and Other Studies.*

Lapp, Eric C. *The Clay Lamps from Ancient Sepphoris: Light Use and Regional Interactions.*

Lipschits, Oded, Yuval Gadot and Liora Freud. *Ramat-Raḥel III: Final Publication of Yohanan Aharoni's Excavations (1954, 1959–1962).* 3 vols.

Owen, David I., with Alexandra Kleinerman. *The Nesbit Tablets.*

Peterson, Ryan S. *The Imago Dei as Human Identity: A Theological Interpretation.*

Porten, Bezalel, and Ada Yardeni. *Textbook of Aramaic Ostraca from Idumea, Volume 2: Dossiers 11–50; 263 Commodity Chits.*

Ristau, Kenneth A., ed. *Reconstructing Jerusalem: Persian Period Prophetic Perspectives.*

Thornton, Dillon T. *Hostility in the House of God: An Investigation of the Opponents in 1 and 2 Timothy.*

Wu, Daniel Y. *Honor, Shame, and Guilt: Social-Scientific Approaches to the Book of Ezekiel.*

Yoder, Tyler R. *Fishers of Fish and Fishers of Men: Fishing Imagery in the Hebrew Bible and the Ancient Near East.*

Zhang, Sarah. *I, You, and the Word "God": Finding Meaning in the Song of Songs.*

2017

Allen, James P. *A Grammar of the Ancient Egyptian Pyramid Texts.* Vol. 1: *Unis.*

Baruchi-Unna, Amitai, Tova Forti, Shmuel Aḥituv, Israel Eph'al, and Jeffrey H. Tigay, eds. *"Now It Happened in Those Days": Studies in Biblical, Assyrian, and Other Ancient Near Eastern Historiography; Presented to Mordechai Cogan on His 75th Birthday.*

Beldman, David J. H. *The Completion of Judges: Strategies of Ending in Judges 17–21.*

Boer, R. de, and J. G. Dercksen, eds. *Private and State in the Ancient Near East: Proceedings of the 58th Rencontre Assyriologique Internationale at Leiden, 16–20 July 2012.*

Dallaire, Hélène M., Benjamin J. Noonan, and Jennifer E. Noonan, eds. *"Where Shall Wisdom be Found?": A Grammatical Tribute to Professor Stephen A. Kaufman.*

Dewrell, Heath D. *Child Sacrifice in Ancient Israel.*

Dothan, Trude, Yosef Garfinkel, and Seymour Gitin. *Tel Miqne 9/1 and 9/3B: The Iron Age IC; Early Philistine City.*

Drewnowska, Olga, and Małgorzata Sandowicz, eds. *Fortune and Misfortune in the Ancient Near East: Proceedings of the 60th Rencontre Assyriologique Internationale at Warsaw 21–25 July 2014.*

Earl, Douglas S. *Reading Old Testament Narrative as Christian Scripture.*

Freedman, Sally M. *If a City Is Set on a Height: The Akkadian Omen Series Shumma Alu ina mele Shakin.* Volume 3: *Tablets 41–6.*

Gitin, Seymour, Trude Dothan, and Yosef Garfinkel. *Tel Miqne 9/2: The Iron Age IIC; Late Philistine City.*

Hasel, Michael G., Yosef Garfinkel, and Shifra Weiss. *Socoh of the Judean Shephelah: The 2010 Survey.*

Heffron, Yağmur, Adam Stone, and Martin Worthington, eds. *At the Dawn of History: Ancient Near Eastern Studies in Honour of J. N. Postgate.* 2 vols.

Herr, Larry G., Douglas R. Clark, and Lawrence T. Geraty, eds. *Madaba Plains Project: The 2000 Season at Tall al-ʿUmayri and Subsequent Studies.*

Holroyd, Kristofer D. *A (S)word against Babylon: An Examination of the Multiple Speech Act Layers within Jeremiah 50–51.*

Jacobs, Paul F., and Joe D. Seger. *Lahav VI: Excavations in Field I at Tell Halif; 1976–1999; The Early Bronze III to Late Arabic Strata.*

Laursen, Steffen, and Piotr Steinkeller. *Babylonia, the Gulf Region, and the Indus: Archaeological and Textual Evidence for Contact in the Third and Early Second Millennium B.C.*

Lipschits, Oded, Yuval Gadot, and Matthew J. Adams, eds. *Rethinking Israel: Studies in the History and Archaeology of Ancient Israel in honor of Israel Finkelstein.*

Lipschits, Oded, Yuval Gadot, Benjamin Arubas, and Manfred Oeming. *What Are the Stones Whispering? Ramat Rahel: 3000 Years of Forgotten History.*

Lipschits, Oded, and Aren M. Maeir, eds. *The Shephelah during the Iron Age: Recent Archaeological Studies.*

Liverani, Mario. *Assyria: The Imperial Mission.*

Moshavi, Adina, and Tania Notarius, eds. *Advances in Biblical Hebrew Linguistics: Data, Methods, and Analyses.*

Patton, Matthew H. *Hope for a Tender Sprig: Jehoiachin in Biblical Theology.*

Spar, Ira, and Michael Jursa. *Cuneiform Texts in The Metropolitan Museum of Art, Volume 4: The Ebabbar Temple Archive and Other Texts from the Fourth to the First Millennium B.C.*

Surls, Austin. *Making Sense of the Divine Name in the Book of Exodus: From Etymology to Literary Onomastics.*

Wikander, Ola. *Unburning Fame: Horses, Dragons, Beings of Smoke, and Other Indo-European Motifs in Ugarit and the Hebrew Bible.*

Witte, Markus. *The Development of God in the Old Testament: Three Case Studies in Biblical Theology.*

.

PHOTO GALLERY

Jim's first year teaching seminary, 1978

Jim, Merna, Johanna, and Gabriel in Redstone, Colorado, for family reunion, 1998

Jim enjoying Halloween at Botanical Garden, October 2013

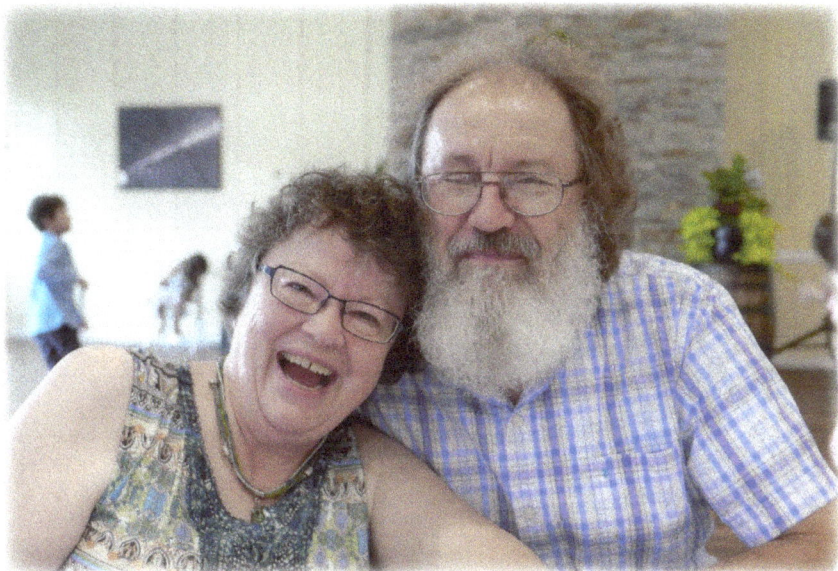

Jim and Merna enjoying Jim's sister's wedding, July 2016

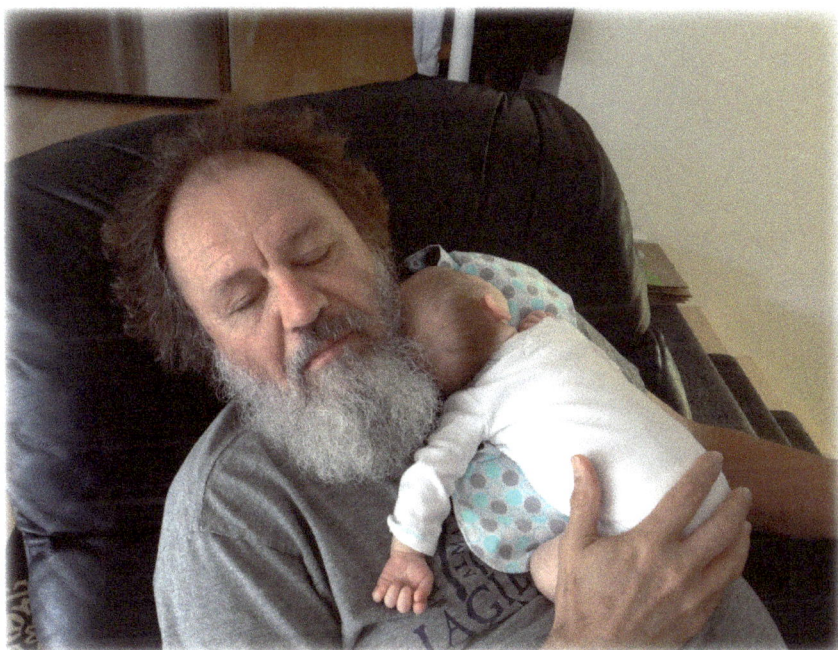

Jim sleeping with new grandson Eli, July 2016

Jim and Merna sharing a dessert during ISBL in Stellenbosch, South Africa, September 2016

Jim, Bruce Waltke, and Michael Patrick O'Connor meeting to plan Eisenbrauns' best-selling book, *Introduction to Biblical Hebrew Syntax* (1989)

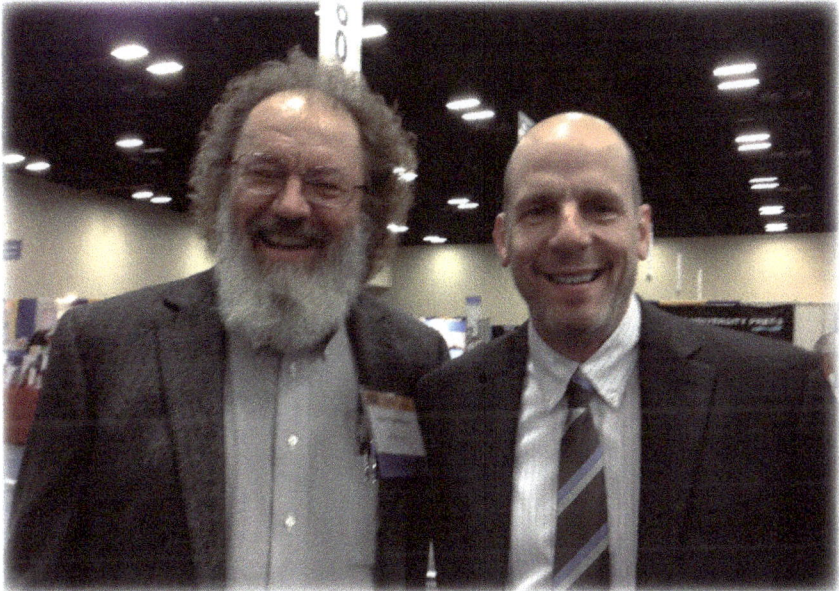

Jim and Jim (Kinney) at SBL in San Diego, November 2016

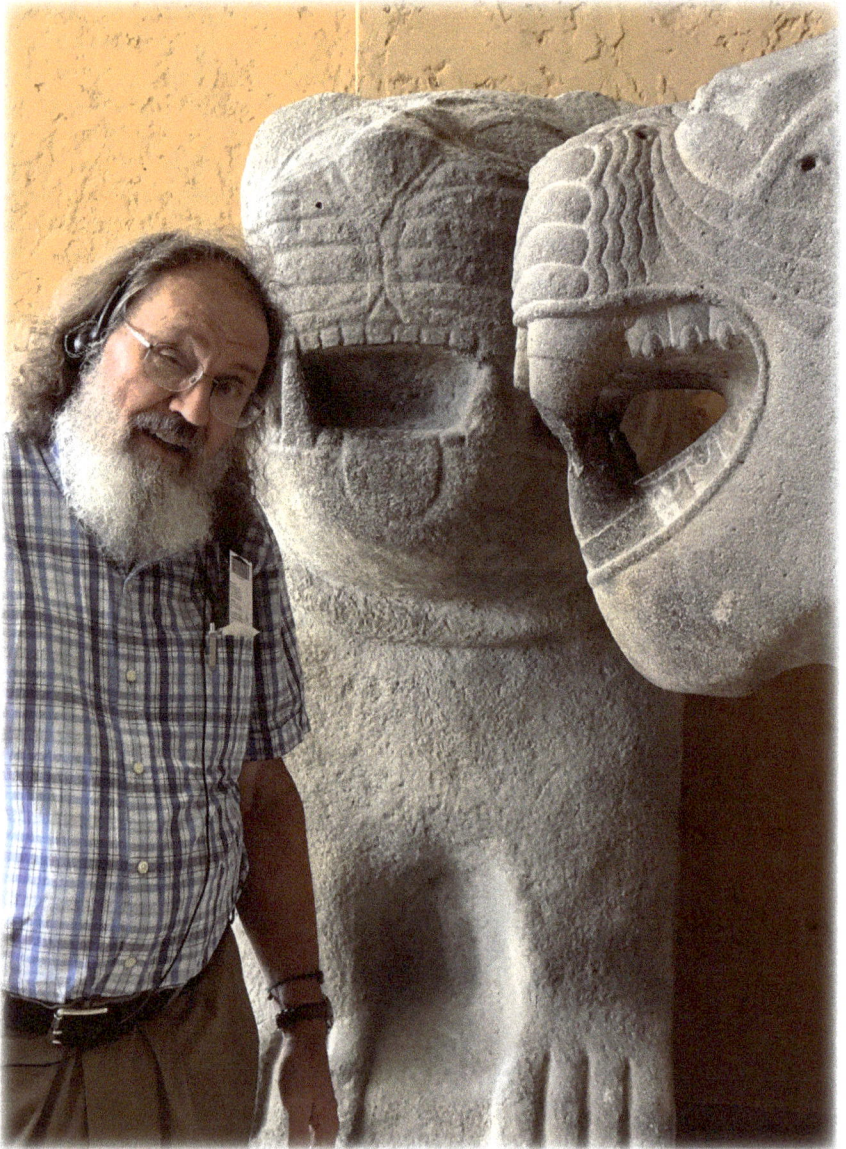

Jim about to be eaten by lions in Berlin, August 2017

Jim making "stone soup" for his church family, September 2017

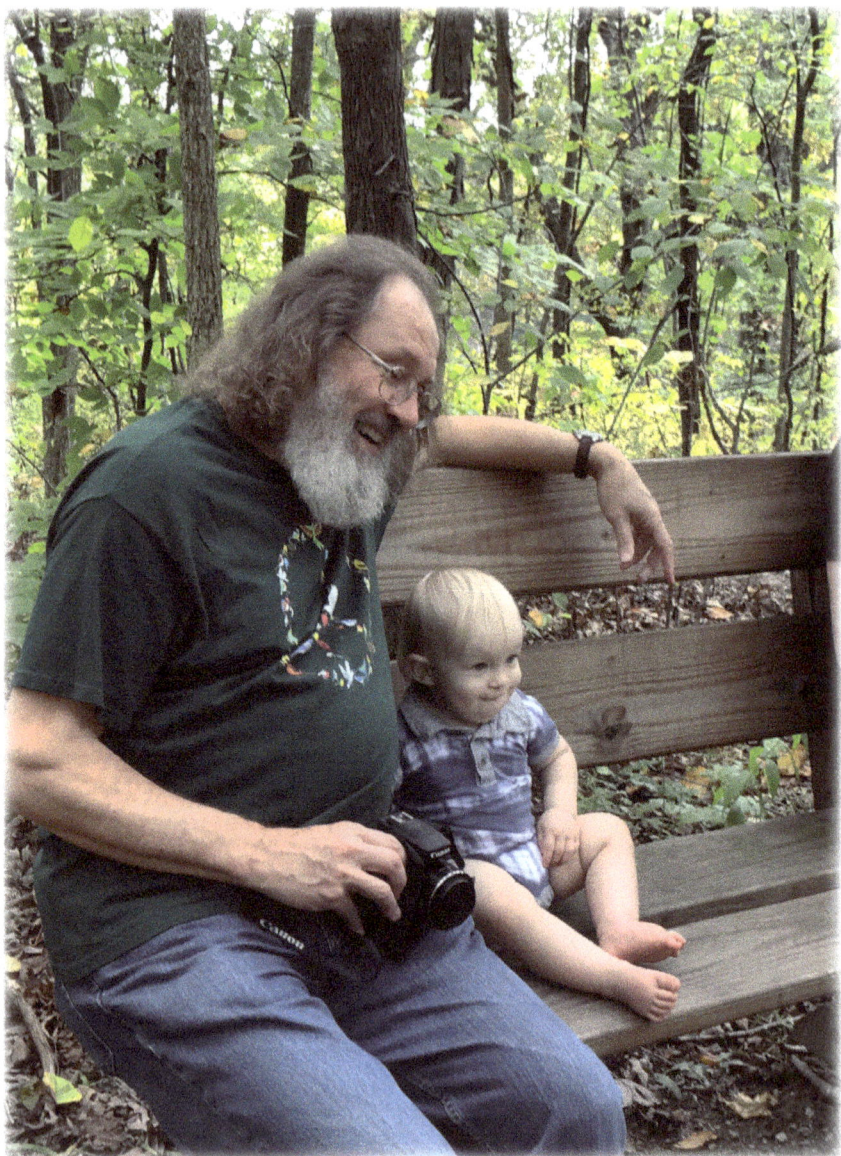

Jim with grandson Eli on family hike for Merna's birthday, October 2017

Jim at the Nowhere Else Festival near Wilmington, Ohio, May 2018

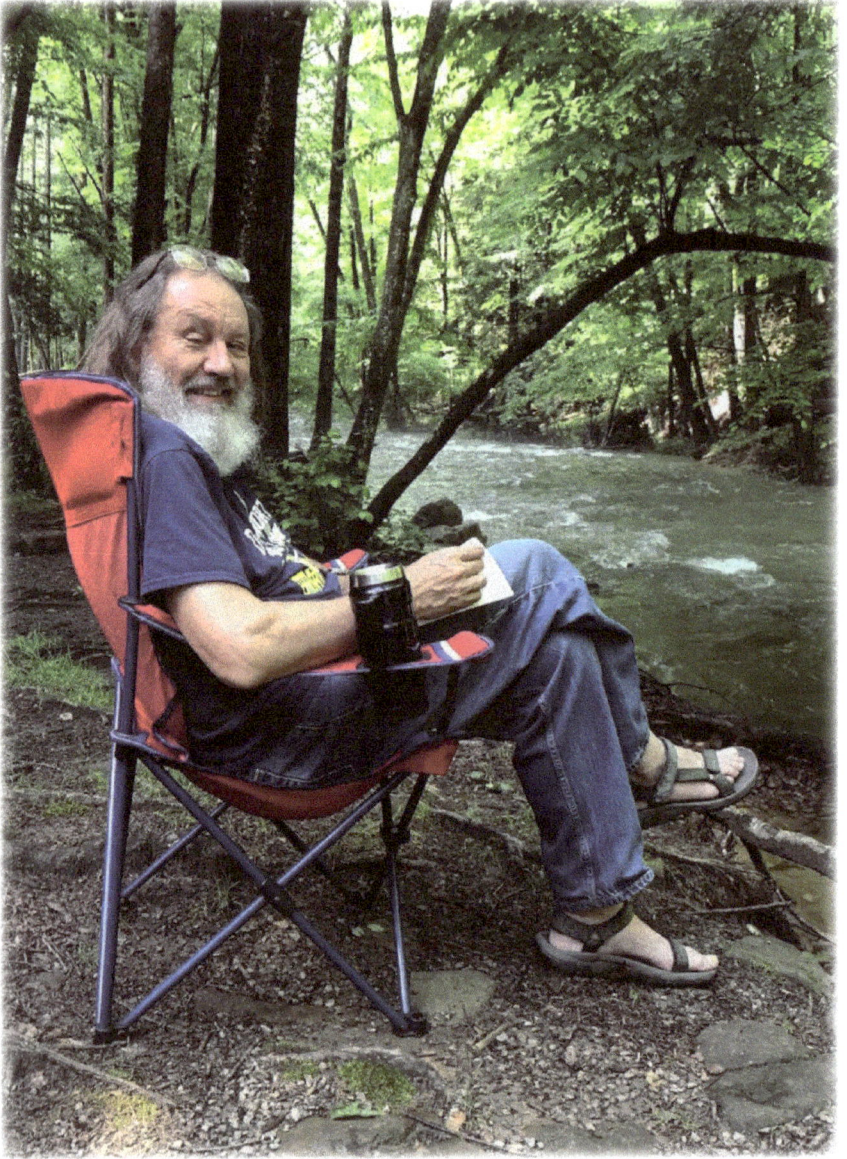

Jim relaxing at Holly River State Park, West Virginia, June 2018

Jim in Aberdeen, Scotland, enjoying a beer, August 2019

Jim enjoying the sunset in Winona Lake, Indiana, September 2019

PERSONAL TRIBUTES

TZVI ABUSCH
Brandeis University

JIM EISENBRAUN INSPIRED AND WORKED WITH MANY SCHOLARS AT ALL stages of their careers and was an intellectual influence and force that we hope will be continued. Two of my volumes were published by Eisenbrauns, a memorial volume for my teacher Thorkild Jacobsen and a volume in which I collected my several essays of interpretation on the Epic of Gilgamesh. Jim urged me to produce the volume on Gilgamesh, something that I might never have done otherwise, and suggested that the work be of a humanistic character. This encouragement is characteristic of Jim's broader approach to antiquity and his belief that scholarship involves not only the examination of details but also includes interpretive work that connects antiquity with our modern world.

Personally, I wish to thank Jim for his encouragement and help and to wish him many years of health and productivity.

SUSAN ACKERMAN
Dartmouth College

AS PRESIDENT OF ASOR, THE AMERICAN SCHOOLS OF ORIENTAL Research, it is a particular honor for me to be able to pay tribute to Jim Eisenbraun on ASOR's behalf, as Jim, through his work as a publisher, has been an invaluable partner to ASOR for more than forty years.

Jim has served ASOR directly by publishing, at one point, the Annual of ASOR book series and by overseeing its publication at others. He also published the now-discontinued series Dissertations of the American Schools of Oriental Research and has managed the production of our flagship journal, the *Bulletin of the American Schools of Oriental Research*. Equally important, Jim has brought forward the final publication of numerous ASOR-affiliated excavated projects and has published countless other monographs by ASOR members.

All Jim's publications, moreover, are of the highest quality and have reflected the highest degree of professionalism. Indeed, he has set the standard for publications in archaeology and in the field of ancient Near Eastern studies. He has also set a standard for distribution, with his commitment to keeping his volumes affordable, so as to disseminate as broadly as possible archaeological, linguistic, historical, and biblical scholarship.

ASOR was honored to be able to recognize the significance of Jim's publishing work by giving him, in 2017, an award for special service to our community. Now, it is my honor, on behalf of ASOR, to laud him again in this collection of tributes, in recognition of the enormous contribution he has made to scholarship in the field of Near Eastern studies.

KAI AKAGI
Japan Bible Seminary

AS RESEARCHERS AND ACADEMIC WRITERS, WE ARE CONTINUALLY indebted to publishers and their staff for the refinement, presentation, and availability of our work. We become acquainted with editors, typesetters, and others who invest in our work through our email exchanges and conversations at conferences, and we develop professional relationships. Among the individuals with whom many in the fields of biblical and ancient Near Eastern studies have developed such a relationship is Jim Eisenbraun. Jim stands out not only through the personal attention and care that he has invested in each volume that Eisenbrauns has published. He has made this investment while being, along with his wife Merna, founder of Eisenbrauns, and while crafting the company into a premier publisher in our fields of research.

In conversations with my co-editors of *Son of God: Divine Sonship in Jewish and Christian Antiquity*, words such as, "I'll write to Jim," "I got an email from Jim," etc., characterized our discussions of matters related to publication, reflecting Jim's personal investment in books and his personal interest and support of us who write and edit them. I am grateful to be able to contribute to this tribute volume for Jim Eisenbraun in thanks for the gift his work has been to students, educators, researchers, and the scholarly community of biblical scholars over the past 40 years and wish him the best for the years to come.

PATRICK H. ALEXANDER
Penn State University Press

WINONA LAKE. RENCONTRE ASSYRIOLOGIQUE INTERNATIONALE. THE 2018 ASOR Special Service Award. *An Introduction to Biblical Hebrew Syntax.* What do these terms have in common? Jim Eisenbraun. Jim would, of course, eschew the encomium that follows, but in my more than thirty-five years of working in scholarly publishing I know of no individual who has had a more formidable and formative publishing presence in an academic discipline. By virtue of his instincts, his publishing program shaped the landscapes of biblical studies, Semitic languages, archaeology, Near Eastern history, literature, and culture. With his enviable command of the material he published, Jim epitomizes the scholar-practitioner. Not only did he know the ancient languages, he knew how to typeset and publish them, and he maintained both his scholarship and his craft at precisely the moment that technology began to disrupt the publishing industry. He adapted, he learned, he persevered in two centuries; and to this day "Eisenbrauns" is synonymous with trusted, cutting-edge scholarship.

With Jim's entrusting the legacy of Eisenbrauns to a new home, Penn State University Press, it will be the responsibility of that press to not only continue the great tradition of producing scholarly resources, but to emulate the intimate relationship that Jim has always had with his authors, his editors, and with his customers. It has been a complete privilege to have worked with Jim closely over the past several years as he shepherded Eisenbrauns to its new home. He and Merna have left a lasting mark both personally and professionally. His is indeed a hard act to follow.

JAVIER ÁLVAREZ-MON
Macquarie University

I MET JIM EISENBRAUN AT THE 2003 CONFERENCE OF THE AMERICAN Schools of Oriental Research in Philadelphia. This event included two sessions dedicated to the rich cultural heritage of ancient Iran and was the first time that Iranian archaeology had been represented at ASOR since the Iranian Revolution. Thanks to Jim's dynamic and personable approach these successful sessions led to the publication of the book *Elam and Persia* (2011, Eisenbrauns; co-edited with Mark B. Garrison). I have remained in touch with Jim throughout the years, enjoying hearing about his frequent trips overseas and sometimes bumping into him at international conferences. I also came to admire his publishing house Eisenbrauns' conscious and professional commitment to the cultures of the ancient Near East, and especially its support for the struggling field of the archaeology and art of ancient Iran, which I represent. Recently, I called at Jim's door seeking advice on the publication of a corpus of Elamite monumental reliefs, a monograph to safeguard an important part of Iran's cultural heritage. Jim's effort and encouragement led to the publication of *The Monumental Reliefs of the Elamite Highlands, A Complete Inventory and Analysis (from the Seventeenth to the Sixth Century BC)* in the prestigious Mesopotamian Civilization series (2018, Eisenbrauns). Jim's imprint on the publishing world offers inspiration against a background of academic presses that have been gradually losing resources and outsourcing editorial skills. Jim's personal commitment to scholarship of the ancient Near East has been a blessing and we owe him a substantial debt of gratitude.

RICHARD E. AVERBECK
Trinity Evangelical Divinity School

I AM DELIGHTED TO WRITE SOMETHING IN HONOR OF MY FRIEND AND colleague Jim Eisenbraun. We have known each other for forty years, even before we taught together at Grace Theological Seminary, beginning in 1980. He had already started his bookstore in Winona Lake, Indiana first as a student at the University of Michigan and then as a professor. He has left a wonderful legacy as one of the scholar publishers who has had substantial impact on the fields of academic biblical and ancient Near Eastern studies.

I remember with gratitude his help in style editing my own dissertation back in the 1980s. I learned a lot about writing and good argument from his feedback. It made my dissertation much better than it would have been otherwise. Since that time, he has encouraged me in my own research and writing and, from time to time, he has called on me for my opinion in some of his publishing projects. I have always found Jim and his good wife Merna engaging. They are good friends.

It has always been a joy to see Jim in all places hither and yon around the world. He has stayed so fully engaged with all that has been going on in the field over the years. His book table was always the one I looked over first at conferences and he was always the one I wanted to see and with whom I wished to converse. It is my hope that he will still be present at some of these events, but it is for sure that his work will be evident.

Jim and Merna, I wish joy together in your retirement. May you and your family prosper in the Lord and in life.

BERNARD F. BATTO
DePauw University

TRANSITIONING FROM BCE TO CE

ONE HAS TO HAVE ACQUIRED A CERTAIN *gravitas*—IN THIS CASE, AGE—
to appreciate the difference between having lived in the period "BCE"
and living now in the period "CE," that is to say, what it was like to have
been a frustrated aspiring scholar in the time "Before the Coming of
Eisenbrauns," as opposed to the joy of finding an eager publisher in
this time of "Celebrating Eisenbrauns." It is indeed with pleasure that
we celebrate the life of Jim Eisenbraun and his work in founding the
publishing enterprise Eisenbrauns, Inc.

Jim Eisenbraun did a great service to the scholarly community when
he conceived Eisenbrauns. Previously, there was little opportunity to
publish the kind of works that Eisenbrauns now publishes so readily.
Prior to Eisenbrauns there were basically three kinds of publishing
houses. At one end of the spectrum were stodgy university presses
like Oxford, Cambridge, Harvard, and the University of Chicago, who
turned out worthy but heavy, carefully researched tomes by established
scholars and often destined primarily for academic libraries. The
polar opposite were popular presses like Harper & Row, Macmillan,
and Doubleday, that catered to the mass market, with an eye primarily upon that bottom line: how well a book would sell and the profits
it would generate. A third type of publisher were the religious presses
like Westminster, Eerdmans, Paulist, and Jewish Publication Society,
focused primarily on disseminating information for specific religious
communities. There was no press available to publish non-religious,
purely academic works that likely would have very limited mass appeal.
Or to put it in more personal terms, there were few publication options
for junior scholars like me, desirous of pairing academic biblical scholarship with ancient Near Eastern studies.

Himself, like me, a young scholar in the early 1970s, Jim Eisenbraun
recognized this lacuna, and the need for a publishing mechanism for
scholarly endeavors falling somewhere between journal-length manu-

scripts and large university presses. In 1975 he founded Eisenbrauns precisely to bridge the scholarly gap between the two disciplines of the ancient Near Eastern studies and academic biblical studies. For me personally, Eisenbrauns under Jim's direction has been a God-send, as it corresponds exactly with my own scholarship goals. To judge from both the quantity and quality of Eisenbrauns publications over the past 40 years, many others have come to a similar conclusion.

Jim is to be lauded not only for recognizing a need but also for persisting in making his enterprise a success. I have no idea whether Eisenbrauns should be considered a commercial success or not. But it most certainly is an academic success, in addition to being a great service in the advancement of biblical scholarship.

Above all, Eisenbrauns is to be commended for the way it trusts its scholar-authors to decide what is publishable and what ought to be published. This is very different from the practice of commercial publishing houses that rely upon an editor or editorial committee to decide whether to publish or not, based upon the expected number of sales. I doubt that any of my three publications with Eisenbrauns would have been accepted using that criterion.

It is with great pleasure,therefore, that I salute Jim Eisenbraun and his many years of wonderful service in the advancement of biblical scholarship.

GARY BECKMAN
University of Michigan

IN ADDITION TO PUBLISHING TWO BOOKS WITH EISENBRAUNS, I HAVE also worked with Jim for twenty years or so as his company has done the prepress work for the *Journal of the American Oriental Society*, for which I serve as Associate Editor for the ancient Near East.

My personal contact with Jim—aside from fairly heavy e-mail traffic—has been limited to scholarly meetings, particularly those of the American Oriental Society. We often sat together at the dinners given for the Editorial Board of the Society's *Journal*, to which Jim was invited as an honorary member. I fondly recall his recollections of graduate study in my Department at the University of Michigan, to which I was called only after his departure for Indiana. Also the amazing tale of his father's trek across Siberia in the late 1940s and his own birding adventures in less exotic climes.

EHUD BEN ZVI
University of Alberta

SCHOLARSHIP AND THE DEVELOPMENT OF NEW KNOWLEDGE REQUIRE infrastructure. Publishers provide an absolutely necessary piece of this infrastructure and great, visionary publishers, like Jim (his wife, "Eisenbrauns" it was and is) make a more significant impact than most scholars in the field. What can I say to him, besides thanks and thanks again, both as a scholar and personally?

I thank you for developing the numerous series you established (and before that for your role as distributor of books), for the excellent editorial support you and yours provided me (and others) over the years, for doing every possible effort to price books as low as possible so as to reduce barriers to scholarship, for publishing volumes from a wide range of perspectives and approaches to enrich the field. I thank you also for all our great conversations, for the projects we worked together, for your constant support over the years, for being always there. Happy retirement and hope to still see you in conferences.

MARIA GIOVANNA BIGA
Sapienza Università di Roma

IT IS A GREAT PLEASURE FOR ME TO EXPRESS MY APPRECIATION FOR JIM
Eisenbraun, a refined publisher, sensitive to all oriental studies research,
even the most innovative, attentive to the diffusion of all the disciplines
of oriental studies, even those that have a more restricted group of
readers.

I have known him for many years and have always appreciated his
discreet and helpful presence at the various Rencontre Assyrioloque
Internationale meetings. Above all, he impressed me a few years ago
on the occasion of a publication that was close to my heart. In 2009,
Mario Liverani, celebrated his 70th birthday and retired from teaching
at Sapienza.

The Department of Historical, Archaeological and Anthropological Sciences of Antiquity, where Mario Liverani had been a leading
specialist since its inception, decided to celebrate his milestone birthday and retirement with a conference held in his honor.

The conference was held in Rome, Sapienza, on April 20–21, 2009.
We invited to Rome a small group of foreign colleagues who represented
the interests of Mario Liverani and his Roman/Italian colleagues. The
title chosen for the meeting was "Not Only History/Non Solo Storia,"
which alludes to Mario Liverani's multiple interests and forays into the
field of the ancient Near East and Egypt.

The scholars invited were: Joaquin Maria Cordoba from Spain,
Johannes Renger from Germany, Irene Winter, Jerrold Cooper, Marc
van De Mieroop, Norman Yoffee, Piotr Michalowski and Peter Machinist from the USA, Jean-Marie Durand and Dominique Charpin from
France, John Baines, David Mattingly and Nicholas Postgate from
England and Nadav Na'aman from Israel. Nicholas Postgate could not
come to Rome but he sent his manuscript later.

The two days of the conference developed into a profitable occasion
for exchanges and discussions among scholars on the highest levels,
and numerous colleagues and students participated.

After the conference, the director of the department, Gilda Bartoloni, and myself, who were the organizers of the conference, were looking for a good publisher who was ready to help us for the volume of its proceedings although we did not have so much money.

Immediately, I suggested asking Jim Eisenbraun!

And, indeed, Jim was very kind and helpful considering both the illustrious Liverani and the level of the conference participants.

He asked us a very favorable price, which the department accepted.

Then the period waiting for contributions and their organization, according to the style requested by the publisher, began.

Some authors sent in their contributions quickly. However, a few extremely busy colleagues delayed and obviously, we preferred to wait for these articles, which were essential to illustrate the activity of Mario Liverani in specific fields.

Jim Eisenbraun was, in this case, very patient for years! Finally, when all the authors had sent their contributions and thanks to the assiduous, patient, and important work of Armando Bramanti, a young Assyriologist who helped the editors adapt all the essays to the style requested by the publisher, we sent them all to Jim Eisenbraun who published it extremely quickly.

The proceedings of the conference were only published in 2016, after considerable delay. Also for this reason, we have to thank Jim Eisenbraun, who trusted and waited for all the articles for years. Finally, he gave me an important suggestion for the title of the volume that was useful for me to understand many things. He suggested putting only "Not Only History" on the book cover, explaining that a title also in Italian would have deterred many possible readers. They would have presumed the presence of articles in Italian, a language difficult to read for many since, unfortunately, Italian failed to become a language for oriental studies. I am also very grateful to Jim Eisenbraun for this suggestion.

ODED BOROWSKI
Emory University

IN THE 1970S JIM WAS A CLASSMATE OF MINE IN GRADUATE SCHOOL AT The University of Michigan, where we shared several classes. I don't remember when I actually met Jim, but I do remember that Jim became associated with bookselling early in our scholarly career. Jim found out that getting textbooks and other books in our field was very hard and expensive. However, he also discovered where to find the books and that purchasing them in quantities lowered the price of individual items. Being enterprising, Jim collected orders from all of us, added a few extra copies to the totals for future students and supplied us with the necessary books.

After being engaged in bookselling for a few years, Jim decided to venture into book publishing. Again, if my recollections serve me right, one of his earliest publications was the first dissertation by a classmate of ours, Michael P. O'Connor, on early Hebrew poetry. Another early publication by Jim was a collection of articles by our esteemed professor David Noel Freedman. It was an important endeavor because these articles were scattered in many publications and mostly unavailable.

I became closely familiar with Jim's publication enterprise when he undertook the publication of my doctoral dissertation *Agriculture in Iron Age Israel*. The book sold out soon, ASOR publications picked up the second edition, and when it was sold out Jim started issuing it on demand as the third edition.

My next encounter with Eisenbrauns press was through the publication of *Lahav III*, in the series of final publications of the Lahav Research Project at Tell Halif. Each volume in the series turned out to be a beautiful piece of work. During the years, Eisenbrauns published numerous books of collected essays to some of which I contributed.

I always enjoyed seeing Jim and his wife Merna at the booksellers display during the ASOR Annual Meetings. Now that they have retired, I hope they continue to attend as regular members and get to relax and enjoy the event without the hassles and pressures of having to sell books. All the best to both of you.

AARON MICHAEL BUTTS
The Catholic University of America

MY STORY IS, I IMAGINE, LIKE MANY OTHERS. AS A GRADUATE STUDENT, I would eagerly peruse the Eisenbrauns book tables at various conferences. This was in fact always the best part of conferences! I aspired to one day have a book there as well. After defending my dissertation and graduating from the University of Chicago, this goal became a reality when a revised version of my dissertation was published by Eisenbrauns. Jim was an integral part of that process: He guided my manuscript from initial submission and peer-review to published book, even graciously spending an entire weekend of his own time to retypeset the many examples in the book. Since the publication of that book, I have remained in regular contact with Jim, peer-reviewing manuscripts for Eisenbrauns and later serving on the editorial board of Eisenbrauns' series Languages of the Ancient Near East (LANE). My relationship with Jim has been long-lasting and rewarding: His work and commitment have left an indelible mark on my career, and for that I am deeply grateful to him.

M. DANIEL CARROLL R. (RODAS)
Wheaton College and Graduate School

ONE OF JIM'S GIFTS IS HIS GRACIOUS SPIRIT. I AM NOT AN ANCIENT Near Eastern specialist, who were the focus of much of Eisenbrauns' publishing. But, Jim's interests are broader than that. I appreciated so much that he would engage me with his smile and encouraged the kind of work that I do, which is largely in the field of Old Testament social ethics and reading the text from minority perspectives. Far from being narrow in his vision, Jim cares about the myriad of ways that scholarship makes the ancient world and the Old Testament intelligible and relevant to modern readers. His is both an academic and faith commitment—a unique combination, indeed. Jim will be missed.

STEPHEN B. CHAPMAN
Duke University

EISENBRAUN APPARENTLY MEANS "IRON BROWN" BY WAY OF MIDDLE
High German and maybe some Yiddish. The usual speculation is that
it referred to someone with a swarthy complexion. It occurs to me that
this surname is practically perfect for a scholar whose work has com-
bined the best of German and Jewish academic scholarship.

Eisenbraun also suggests fortuitous associations for me. I think of
how since 1975 Eisenbrauns, the house that Jim built, has served a cru-
cial role as an independent publisher offering a platform for the very
best work in biblical studies—for over 40 years, then, an Eisenzeit or
"Iron Age." The creation and maintenance of such an institution never
happens by accident. It takes a huge amount of effort by ein Mann aus
Eisen or "a man of iron," someone who perpetually and characteristically has mehrere Eisen im Feuer or "more than one iron in the fire."
More personally, the word Eisenbraun makes me think as well of a
Braunbär or "brown bear," especially since Jim has always struck me
as a bear of a guy. He has a "brawny" presence, physically and mentally
and spiritually. He has the curiosity of a bear too, always seeking and
reading and learning. Then perhaps like Smokey the Bear, he has also
been a guide, an encourager, and a mentor to so many. But Jim is ever
the honest broker, able to deliver disappointing news in a manner that
is compassionate yet forthcoming and firm. He knows that the fundamental task of the publisher is to make judgments.

Our cultural moment is not kind to builders or institutions. It is
always easier to tear things down. But as a "man of iron," Jim has instead
used his considerable strength to build up. His legacy will continue to
serve the academy and the church for many years to come. It has been
my joy to collaborate with him, to learn from him, and to share in the
benefits of his prodigious labors. It has been wonderful in particular
to see Siphrut, the monograph series I co-edit with Tremper Longman
and Nathan MacDonald, move through the initial stages of pipe dream,
phone calls, and drawing board to its current realization: 25 volumes

now in print and more on the way, still appearing as an Eisenbrauns imprint with Pennsylvania State University Press.

JOHN A. COOK
Asbury Theological Seminary

IT IS A PLEASURE TO CONTRIBUTE TO THIS VOLUME OF REFLECTIONS ON
Jim Eisenbrauns and his contribution to biblical and ancient Near Eastern studies. I count it a privilege to have had a connection with Jim and
the Eisenbrauns enterprise from a number of different angles over the
years—from coveting their books that I could not yet afford as a graduate student, to working for Jim as an acquisitions editor for a short
time, to publishing my own works with them.

I recall during my masters program in Chicagoland traveling back
to New Jersey and convincing my wife Kathy to take a detour to visit
Eisenbrauns. It felt a surreal to walk around the corner shelf of Eisenbrauns publications and be able to peruse them in the place where they
were produced, in that very unassuming building in Warsaw Indiana.

For as brief as my time was working at Eisenbrauns and living in
Winona Lake Indiana, it developed to the greatest extent my fond-
ness for and admiration of Jim Eisenbraun and his significance to our
fields. I don't think there is another publisher who is as passionate and
invested in his publications as Jim has been for over forty years! When
I joined Jim and his company, they were already well-respected fixtures
in the field, and yet Jim was and continues to be self-effacing and gracious with both his authors and his employees.

Jim's unique combination of serious passion for the work and graciousness towards his employees made the Eisenbrauns workplace
close to family, if not also a motley crew. During my short time at
Eisenbrauns, birthday celebrations, pranks, rubber-band fights, as well
as Greek and Hebrew reading sessions and rich personal conversations
were interspersed with the meticulous work of producing books out
of manuscripts. Though old enough to be my father, Jim graciously
treated me as his colleague, respecting my advice, introducing me to
well-established authors in the field, and having me accompany him
to meetings. My trip to the International SBL meetings in Edinburgh
in 2006 was less memorable for the meetings than it was for spending
time touring and getting to know Jim.

My departure from Eisenbrauns back into teaching was accompanied by a degree of sadness, and the acquisition of Eisenbraun as an imprint of Penn State University Press and Jim's stepping back from the business has brought nostalgic recollections of working with Jim. I will confess what many others may echo: that every SBL meeting I make my way to the Eisenbrauns booth first, knowing that anything they publish will be worth looking at, and only then (if I have any more room or money for books) do I go perusing the other book sellers in the hall.

To have had the privilege, after so long admiring Eisenbrauns from afar, to both participate in Jim's business as acquisitions editor—be it ever so briefly—and to have my own works included among their publications, will always remain highlights of my academic career.

JERRY COOPER
Johns Hopkins University/UC Berkeley

IN THE MID-1980S, DISCUSSIONS WITH SEVERAL COLLEAGUES REVEALED the need for a new monograph series for works in Assyriology and related disciplines. The economies of academic publishing in the U.S. had been gradually shrinking the pool of publishers with which one could place the kind of work we offered: books with limited marketability and complicated to produce--lots of special characters, copious footnotes, citations in many languages. European monograph series were still accessible, but their prices were astronomical. There was, however, one American publisher that had demonstrated great competence in producing scholarly books on the ancient Near East at very reasonable prices: Eisenbrauns!

When I approached Jim with a proposal to start up Mesopotamian Civilizations, he was enthusiastic and supportive. I especially appreciated his agreement that we provide honorariums to reviewers of manuscripts. Working with Jim was always a pleasure, despite some timing glitches with *earlier* volumes. What has resulted from our engagement is a series of handsomely produced, affordable monographs that expand our knowledge of Mesopotamian civilizations. I am confident that it will continue to be so, under the aegis of Pennsylvania State University Press, and with the direction of the new General Editor of the series, Jacob Lauinger.

The most memorable volume Jim and I turned out was Jean Bottéro's *Textes culinaires mésopotamiens* in 1995. Jean was a demanding, if congenial, author, and used copious amounts of white-out and correction tape on both his original manuscript and subsequent proofs. I especially remember one thick envelope with corrected proofs that arrived soaked through by rain encountered somewhere between Gif and Baltimore. The water had loosened the correction tape and smeared the white-out, and figuring out what corrections went where was quite a job. But, in the end, Jim produced a beautiful volume with a full-color image of one of the Yale culinary tablets as frontispiece, and which, if I remember correctly, outsold all other books in the series.

That volume won the 1996 Langhe Cerretto Prize, given "for the best work dealing with topics relating to the historical, scientific, dietological, gastronomical or sociological aspects of food and wine." Jim generously brought me along to Alba in the Langhe region of Italy for several glorious days of celebration at the Cerretto winery, when he and Jean were awarded the prize, and he formed a fast friendship with Jean. It was an experience I will never forget, and neither, I'm sure, will Jim.

Jim's decades-long contribution to ancient Near Eastern studies has been profound and invaluable. I join his many collegues in wishing him a long and enjoyable well-earned retirement!

MARTI DAHLQUIST
Eisenbrauns, Operations Manager, 2000–2014; Customer Service,
1996–2000

I CANNOT SPEAK TO THE IMPACT JIM HAD ON THE ACADEMIC WORLD,
because I was not an academic scholar. I could repeat the accolades
said to me, over and over, while interacting with students and professors at conferences or while responding to customer service inquiries.
There was never a shortage of gratitude expressed for Jim's vision of a
press that provided quality titles at affordable prices. Anything in the
academic arena though, I'd be a secondhand witness.

I experienced Jim Eisenbraun as an employee. Twenty minutes
after my last final in college I had my second interview at Eisenbrauns
and was offered my first job after college. What started as an entry-
level receptionist position launched an eighteen-year career that would
transition me to customer service manager and would shape me as an
employee. At the heart of my professional journey was my boss, Jim,
who set an insanely high bar for future bosses to come.

Jim did not see employees as one-dimensional assets for the business to utilize. He saw employees as vibrant, fluid, sometimes broken,
symbiotic beings who were most productive in their work when all
aspects of their lives were functioning optimally. He cared deeply about
his employees. On my transition to management, Jim carved time out
of his schedule to meet with me for about an hour, sometimes weekly
sometimes biweekly. It was an hour where I had his full attention and
there was never a specific agenda other than what I felt like I needed
from him at that moment. He would cheer on, encourage, reveal areas
that needed improvement, listen, and help me sort out my path as a
new manager.

One meeting had little to do with traditional work. I had just had
to put a pet to sleep for the first time, a decision that was personally
devastating and hard to understand the responsibility involved when it
came to end of life decisions. Jim let me spend our meeting time griev-
ing and talking out my internal struggle. From a business perspective
the hour had nothing to do with selling books. Jim knew enough about

how humans operate, though, to know that by helping me put myself back together, he was sending out a stronger, more stable employee in the long run.

Jim's impact on my development as an employee goes beyond my time at Eisenbrauns. I'm now in my second career and am a registered nurse. There is not a shift that goes by where I do not hear Jim's advice running through my head. Patients that Jim will never meet are reaping the benefits of his personal and professional investment in me. Jim taught me how to be a good employee, but more importantly he showed me how to be a better "me," which is a legacy that will have impact beyond our eighteen professional years spent together.

PETER T. DANIELS
independent scholar

IN THE LATER 1970S, THE EDITORIAL OFFICE OF THE CHICAGO ASSYRIAN Dictionary handled the occasional order from individuals for copies of the volumes; I joined the staff in 1976. If a complete set was ordered, a request was sent to the Museum Preparator, and in a day or so he would appear with a securely wrapped set trundled on a cart. Some of those parcels, we noted, were being ordered by an unfamiliar bookseller in Ann Arbor, Michigan, by the name of Eisenbrauns, and naturally these were billed at the wholesale discount price. But was this a legitimate bookseller or a gimmick by creative Assyriology students to pay a lower price than was set by the publisher? I was tasked with verifying Eisenbrauns' *bona fides*, and my first inquiry brought by return mail a brief catalog—one page, perhaps—of books offered for sale by one Jim Eisenbraun. He may at that time have already acquired the rights to reprint a handful of recent classic titles in the field, such as Albright's *Yahweh and the Gods of Canaan* and Wright's *Bible and the Ancient Near East*.

I do not know when I first met Jim Eisenbraun, whether at a North American Conference on Afroasiatic Linguistics, an annual joint meeting of the Midwest Region of the SBL, the AOS, and ASOR, or some other conference. Any one of those venues could have been the fateful location. What was important was that Jim had begun publishing original books in biblical and Near Eastern studies. Among the first was Michael Patrick O'Connor's *Hebrew Verse Structure* (1980). It was at a Midwest meeting that Jim introduced me to Michael, who became my closest friend—my lifelong friend, as it turned out.

As an Anglophone student of Semitic languages, I felt a much unneeded gap in basic texts about Proto-Semitic. English works were few, and what might be considered the finest of all such overviews, Gotthelf Bergsträßer's *Einführung*, is highly compressed and often quite difficult. It occurred to me that the only way to be able to read it would be to write out a translation.

After I completed the translation, it occurred to me that it could be useful to others, and I approached Jim Eisenbraun; he agreed to take on the publication. Perhaps he didn't know quite what he was getting into, for it further occurred to me that it would be useful if the original orthographies of the text specimens were included, and that would necessitate an added chapter on the scripts of the Semitic languages. Never did Jim demur, even when it became necessary to appproach typesetters on two continents to accomplish that goal, and never did Jim complain about the expense!

My experience with the competence of Jim and his staff led me to introduce him to L. Paula Woods, long-time Assistant Editor, later Managing Editor, of the *Journal of Near Eastern Studies*, and Johannes Renger of the Oriental Institute, Ancient Near East Section Editor of the *Journal of the American Oriental Society*. Both were looking for more efficient typesetting; the former led to relationships with other University of Chicago Press journals, the latter to a continuing association and the publication of many volumes of the American Oriental Series from all five sections of the Society.

The latter capacity led to an another occasion for me to call on Eisenbrauns' printing ability. *The World's Writing Systems*, which I coedited with William Bright, was created in the days before Unicode font-encoding was generally available and before pdf files could be generated from within a word processor. When it turned out that neither I nor the publisher could create pdfs of these pages from which camera-ready copy could be produced, we were able to call upon Eisenbrauns for this specialized task. This achievement was reciprocated when Jim called on me to typeset Patrick Bennett's manual of comparative Semitic.

The Bergsträßer translation led Jim to call on me for further translations, including a number of chapters for volumes in the Sources for Biblical and Theological Study series, Pierre Briant's history of the Achaemenid Empire, and the long-delayed *Creation* by Othmar Keel and Sylvia Schroer (2015).

At some point in the 1980s, Jim Eisenbraun asked me to referee the manuscript of a short monograph with which I vigorously disagreed (yet still recommended publication). Jim Eisenbraun did not enter into the long epistolary conversation that ensued. He has remained always a calm presence at the heart of a wealth of publications in biblical and Oriental studies, controlling always for quality and maintaining increasingly rare standards of the art of the book, himself designing the typography of many of the striking interiors. He has been a treasure in the field for going on half a century.

HEATH D. DEWRELL
Princeton Theological Seminary

JIM EISENBRAUN HAS BEEN INSTRUMENTAL IN MY OWN SCHOLARSHIP in two important ways. First, he and his publishing house have produced indispensable resources that I could afford to add to my library even as a poor graduate student. A high proportion of the books in my library still bears little ibexes (ibices?) on the spine. Secondly, Jim was instrumental in the publication of my revised dissertation. Having had no prior experience with publishing a book, I now realize that the manuscript that I turned in needed a more work and care than most editors would prefer. Jim personally served as editor on my manuscript and was wonderfully patient and encouraging, graciously working with me through several drafts without airing any of the complaints that he had every right to air. In many ways, Jim was as important for my academic growth as a young scholar as many of my graduate professors. Having talked with colleagues in the field, I know that my experience with Jim in this regard is far from unique. The field of Near Eastern Studies is a far better place for his having been in it, and we all owe Jim an enormous debt of gratitude.

NANCY ERICKSON
Zondervan Academic

AS A YOUNG ACADEMIC I KNEW ONLY OF A PUBLISHING *house* NAMED Eisenbrauns, not of a person Jim Eisenbrauns that lay behind the esteemed business. Early entry into studies of biblical Hebrew found me owning, referencing, and wrestling with *Introduction to Biblical Hebrew Syntax*, still a standard in language studies and published by Eisenbrauns in its early years. It is one of many exceptional Eisenbrauns publications that have shaped my studies and those of countless others. At the time of my PhD work I was unaware that I would later find myself working for an academic publisher, editing original content, pursuing prolific authors, and living into the academy. So, from one editor to another, Jim, I applaud your many, many hours of dream-casting, styling, laboring over minutia, and producing the best of the best.

Cheers, my friend, to outstanding work and a beautiful legacy!

WALTER FARBER
The Oriental Institute, The University of Chicago

JIM EISENBRAUN STARTED HIS SPECIALIZED BOOKSELLING BUSINESS IN Michigan in 1975, and "Eisenbrauns" quickly became a synonym for affordable books in ancient Near Eastern studies on both sides of the Atlantic. No other bookseller could match Eisenbrauns' prices on the European market for scholarly books published in America, and after Jim added his own publishing program to the portfolio a few years later, every scholar in the broader field of Near Eastern and biblical Studies in Europe and elsewhere knew his catalogues, name, and business address.

I got my PhD in Tübingen in Germany in 1973 and started my academic career as a *Wissenschaftlicher Assistent* at the München university in early 1974. One of the major tasks of this position was to maintain the Institute's library by making the best use of its nice but still limited budget. No wonder that I soon discovered the new enterprise from Ann Arbor, which happened also to be a partner city of my home town of Tübingen, and that already in 1976 Jim could count the *Institut für Assyrologie* in Munich among his regular customers.

In 1980, my wife Gertrud and myself moved to the University of Chicago, and my business relationship with Jim as a bookseller was for the following decades reduced to the much smaller budget of maintaining my own private library. During these years, I also first met Jim personally at one of the AOS meetings, beginning a tradition that would continue for many years to come. At one of these meetings, in the mid-1980ies, I was also asked by Jerry Cooper, whether I would like to join the editorial board of a new series of peer-reviewed high class publications called "Mesopotamian Civilizations" which he was planning to inaugurate, and which would be published by Eisenbrauns. I readily agreed, and have served on that board ever since, first under the leadership of Jerry, and then with my former student Jake Lauinger at the helm. With this decision came some major changes in my relationship with Jim: As co-editor of a flagship series, I in a way now also worked directly for his publishing firm. But at the same time Jerry and Jim convinced me to publish my next book, "Schlaf, Kindchen, Schlaf!" in just this series. This was not such an easy decision, since the manuscript was in German and originally meant for publication in Germany. Publishing a book in the USA in a foreign language was also considerd quite a marketing risk. But we agreed to try it anyway, and through this process, I also got to work closely with Jim as an editor: although officially somebody else was assigned to take care of me and my editorial problems, Jim was always the person to step in if needed, especially when language-specific problems arose. He later told me that the book actually had noticeably lower sales figures than comparable titles in English, but he never gave me the feeling that he regretted having published it in German. Maybe he also thought it added a little international flair to an otherwise mostly English publication program.

Jumping ahead over 20 years, around 2010, my final major Assyriological project, the edition of the Lamaßtu text corpus in monographic form, came closer to fruition, and again Jerry Cooper and Jim stepped in to convince me to publish it in "Mesopotamian Civilizations." This time, however, Jim made it clear that he wanted it to be in English. In return, he offered me to act as my personal editor of the book, if I consented to let him publish it. And so it happened. After I had finally finished the manuscript in 2011, and then had the text editions proofread against the cuneiform copies and my English corrected by a grad student in early 2012, a year of very intensive cooperation with Jim began. After initial struggles with my antiquated fonts and software, the most daunting task was to edit the score transliterations. In an almost daily exchange of emails, together we went through all of these page by page, until finally all spacings, vertical alignments etc. were in place. Jim, true to his original promise, did basically all the editing and correcting himself, and on the few occasions that somebody else had tried to make some corrections, which regularly had to be undone by Jim, it became crystal clear to me what luck I had had in securing his personal attention and know-how. The book was to be presented at my retirement celebration in early 2013, and Jim had promised to come to Chicago himself and make the presentation, but alas, last minute family problems prevented him from coming, and we had to celebrate without him. This is even more regrettable, since it prevented me once more from finally having a quiet beer with Jim. Believe it or not, in 45 years of business relationship and professional cooperation, and in spite of the countless meetings we both attended, he as a businessman and I as a scholarly participant, we never got a chance to seal our friendship in this way. What a shame!

STEVEN E. FASSBERG
The Hebrew University of Jerusalem

AS A GRADUATE STUDENT AT THE END OF THE 1970S AND BEGINNING of the 1980s, I first heard of Jim Eisenbraun from a teacher who mentioned that one could order books printed in Europe through a catalogue put out by someone named Jim Eisenbraun. I got myself onto the Eisenbrauns mailing list and every new issue of the catalogue made me feel like a child in a candy store.

A few years later I saw that the same Jim Eisenbraun was now publishing books. I got on the mailing list again and the next thing I knew I was buying lots of books that Eisenbrauns was publishing. The books were aesthetically printed and produced and within a short time Eisenbrauns became a leading publisher of books dealing with Bible and the ancient Near East, successfully competing with and often surpassing older European publishers. At an SBL meeting in the States I finally got to meet the legendary Jim Eisenbraun standing at the Eisenbrauns table. I was a bit taken a back when I realized that I was talking with Jim Eisenbraun himself. He was soft-spoken, warm,and friendly. He reminded me at first blush more of Paul Bunyan than the publishing magnate that I expected. He was and is a gentle giant in more ways than one.

My first professional contact with Jim was when I was involved with the final editing of the English translation of Ze'ev Ben-Ḥayyim's *Grammar of Samaritan Hebrew* (2000). Magnes Press co-published the volume with Eisenbrauns. My second experience was when Magnes Press co-published with Eisenbrauns a volume that Avi Hurvitz and I edited entitled *Biblical Hebrew in Its Northwest Semitic Setting: Typological and Historical Perspectives* (2006). A third work-related experience was when Eisenbrauns published a two-volume work that W. Randall Garr and I edited, *A Handbook of Biblical Hebrew* (2016). The most recent contact with Jim was at a dinner hosted by Craig Morrison, O. Carm, with others on the roof of a Carmelite monastery during the most recent international SBL (2019) in Rome.

Jim Eisenbraun is one of the kindest, gentlest, most down-to-earth, sensible, efficient, and talented people that I have ever met. Every interaction with him, be it by letter, email, or in person, has always been with a smile, with a laugh, and with much goodwill. You don't expect that kind of treatment from a man who single-handedly built a publishing empire and in doing so left a huge imprint on the quality and quantity of research into the Bible and the ancient Near East.

AVRAHAM FAUST
Bar-Ilan University

I FIRST MET JIM WHEN I STARTED ATTENDING THE ASOR (AND SBL) Annual Meetings—the first one was in 2001, just after finishing my PhD. Eisnbrauns Publishing was well established at this time, and always had a large booth at the conference (where, I must confess, rather than at the lecture-halls, I spent too much time…).

As I became more immersed in the field, I learned that one has to choose carefully where to publish, in order to reach the right audience. It became clear that if one wanted to reach Near Eastern archaeologists in particular, and scholars of Near Eastern studies in general, Eisenbrauns is the best avenue, and I can say with certainly that no book that is published by Eisenbrauns can be missed by anyone in these fields!

I published many articles in Eisenbrauns's volumes over the years, and when I decided to have an updated, English edition of my PhD (published in Hebrew by Yad Ben-Zvi), Eisenbrauns was a natural choice. Jim's handling of the book—*The Archaeology of Israelite Society in Iron Age II* (2012)—was very efficient and professional, and the final product was excellent (in my, not most objective, view). Jim was very cooperative in all matters related to the book, review copies, etc.

More recently, when Shawn Aster and myself wanted to publish our edited volume on *The Southern Levant Under Assyrian Domination* (2018), Eisenbrauns was again the natural choice. This was at the time when Eisnebrauns was making the transition to Pennsylvania State University Press, and some of my colleagues expressed concerned that it will delay the publication. This, however, was not the case, and the entire process was very efficient and fast, and both the contributors and some of the colleagues (who didn't contribute) were surprised by the speedy publication process and the quality of the results.

All in all, Jim created an empire—Eisenbrauns appears to have become the best publishing venue for Near Eastern Studies—and very few people can boast such an achievement!

Personally, I should add that over the years I benefited from Jim's wisdom and advice on various delicate professional issues, for which I am of course also grateful. For your contribution to the field, and for your cooperation and help, Jim, Many Thanks!

ISRAEL FINKELSTEIN
Tel Aviv University

IF JIM WERE WITH US HERE IN ISRAEL TODAY WE WOULD LIFT A GLASS
and say L'Chaim to him for a job well done and for many years of
friendly cooperation. Over the years, we have collaborated on a number
of projects: Jim produced several of our Tel Aviv University Institute of
Archaeology's Monograph Series, for which I serve as editor; He published festschrifts for my colleagues and friends Nadav Naaman and
David Ussishkin—in both I served as co-editor; and recently he produced a festschrift in my honor, titled Rethinking Israel. And of course,
throughout the years I wrote a number of articles in books which were
published by Eisenbrauns. All along Jim's work was highly professional
and his attitude always friendly and forthcoming. His imprint is in my
scholarship and in the books of the Institute in many ways.

A. DEAN FORBES
University of the Free State

IT HAS BEEN NEARLY FOUR DECADES SINCE FIRST I LEARNED OF JIM
Eisenbraun, he the publisher and I the part-time student of the Hebrew
Bible. There were always intermediaries in those early days: David Noel
Freedman and Francis Andersen. While they occasionally lamented
that Jim was so busy, my two mentors unwaveringly held him in very
high regard. Our tremendous esteem continued down the decades.

My earliest recollection of one-on-one interactions with Jim dates
to the early nineties when Freedman, Andersen, and I were writing and
making "camera-ready" *Studies in Hebrew and Aramaic Orthography*.
My contributions involved formatting and preparing the manuscript
and writing several tough-sledding (for biblical scholars) chapters
involving statistical concepts. While I was urged to make the material
as accessible as possible (well, דוה!), I was not obliged to "For Dum-
mies-ize" it, a stance that I have always appreciated.

Two decades later, I presented Jim with what I considered the
"publication-ready manuscript" of Frank Andersen's and my book on
grammar, *Biblical Hebrew Grammar Visualized*. In short order and
with no hint of condescension, Jim himself showed what true a pro
could bring to a manuscript. He, and later Beverly McCoy, went over
the entire manuscript, greatly improving this layout-challenging book.

Over the years, Jim and I have developed a quasi-tradition of sharing a breakfast at the annual SBL meetings (and sometimes dinner with
our wives, Merna and Ellen). I have come to treasure our shared meals,
always interludes of serious, direct, and uplifting conversation.

I will miss the customary interactions with Jim. However, since we
share membership on the board of the non-profit that now owns the
Andersen-Forbes database, I anticipate many future exchanges.

TOVA FORTI
Ben-Gurion University of the Negev

JIM EISENBRAUN HAS BEEN A LIGHTHOUSE IN THE ACADEMIC CROSSROAD
of many biblical scholars. During my research I was happy to contribute
occasionally papers for festschrifts dedicated to colleagues and mentors.
This particular genre gained the highest meticulous and eloquent care of
our honoree. Jim always insisted on producing a subject-focused volume
of qualified papers. The high quality of the paper and print and the elegant design of the cover provided these books the appropriate status on
the shelf of every respectable academic library. The name Eisenbrauns
rightfully gained the prestige of high quality of research.

My most significant prerogative of working with Jim was during
the process of publication of the Festschrift dedicated to Mordechai
Cogan (2017) of which I was one of the editors. Jim was personally
involved in every stage of its preparation. His academic persona that
combines expertise in Bible, Archaeology and ancient Near Eastern
studies dominated the final result of this two volumes Festschrift.

Correspondence with Jim was always a pleasure. No high words, no
arrogance, just straightforward professional guidance. His personality
inspired a strong sense of credibility and collaboration that made any
person with whom he corresponded to become a partner and friend.

I was lucky again to enjoy the collaboration with Jim when my
monograph *Like a Lone Bird on a Roof": Animal Imagery and the
Structure of Psalms* (Critical Studies in the Hebrew Bible 10; eds. A.C.
Hagedorn, N. McDonald, and S. Weeks) was accepted for publication
(2018) by Eisenbrauns. Words of encouragement were an integral part
of the process of the production of my book, For example:

> *I'm delighted to hear of the extensive work that you've already done on
> the book; it appears to be thorough and very well done, and I congratu-
> late you for this: it's not a minor achievement!*

And even when some misunderstanding occurred with regard the
information on the cover of the book due to the move of Eisenbrauns to

the press of Penn State University, Jim was still the person with whom I could share my concern. His personal and professional attention is best illustrated in his letter cited below:

> *If I may, just a word about the way that the copy on the back of the book functions. It is useful to have information about the book on the back; and everyone (including us) wants to make it as accurate and inviting as possible. That the process wasn't followed quite as it should have been in this case is unfortunate. And I know that PSU Press is revising the information for the website and will post an update fairly soon, to reflect the information that you had provided.*
>
> *I've not yet seen a copy of the book myself; however, I can tell you that the back of the book will not be seen by many before they purchase it. Most sales will happen through the website or to libraries; thus, the information about the book that's on the back cover won't influence sales very much (or, therefore, be misleading to very many people at all). Perhaps the main place that potential readers will actually read the back of the book prior to purchasing will be at conferences (based, at least, on my experience through the years). So, from my perspective, the problem, although disconcerting, is not especially fatal. And at the same time, it would be extremely economically difficult to justify halting distribution now; as Jennifer has noted, any reprints will have the corrected copy, and it seems to me that that will mitigate the problem sufficiently. This at least is my perspective on the matter, for what it's worth.*
>
> *Personally, I'm very much looking forward, too, to seeing the book itself!*
>
> *Warmly,*
> *Jim Eisenbraun*

The same spirit of constant care and attention is expressed in his latest note of congratulations after a RBL of my book was published.

Reflecting on Jim Eisenbraun's contribution to our academic world brings to mind ancient librarians such as Demetrius Phalerum, the originator of the universal library in Alexandria—in a parallel vein, Jim dedicated his life to foster and cultivate scholarship offering the most prestigious academic stage.

NILI FOX
Hebrew Union College, Cincinnati

YOU COULD ALWAYS COUNT ON JIM'S HEARTY WELCOME WHEN STOPPING
by Eisenbruans' booth at SBL meetings. As hectic as business was around
him, Jim always made time to talk, whether about the progress of your
publication, the nature of ancient Near Eastern and biblical studies, or
opportunities for your students who were anxious to publish a first book.
    Since I advise multiple Ph.D. dissertations, Jim and his team would
consult with me about publishing manuscripts of new HUC-JIR Ph.D.s.
In the past two decades more than a dozen of our alums published their
first books with Eisenbrauns. Topics vary: philological studies, ancient
Near Eastern astronomy, children in the ancient world, the biblical wilderness accounts, Jewish liturgy, and others.
    Eisenbrauns' publications feature a library of books on a range of
fields, each reflecting the value Jim placed on such scholarly works.
Festchrifts, often unwelcome to publishers, also found a home with
Eisenbrauns. I served as an editor and contributor to one, giving me
a chance to work closely with Jim and his team. It was a pure delight,
even affording us the opportunity to design the book's cover.
    I wish Jim many healthy and fulfilling years ahead. Be proud of
your contributions to biblical and ancient Near Eastern studies and
keep smiling.

R. MICHAEL FOX
Southwestern Christian University

JIM EISENBRAUN HAS BEEN INVOLVED IN PUBLISHING SOME OF THE most advanced works in biblical studies over the last few decades. That said, he still found a place for an unknown author like myself and a niche book like mine simply because he and his team thought it needed to be published. To my surprise and delight, Jim and I ended up talking roots music in our professional correspondences! Jim is one of a kind, and we who are tied to academic publishing in biblical studies are grateful for his contributions and unique persona.

GRANT FRAME
University of Pennsylvania

I CANNOT RECALL WHEN I FIRST MET JIM, BUT I DO HAVE RECORDS OF ordering from Eisenbrauns going back to the late 1970s and I remember being very happy to find a place from which I could order most of the books that I wanted for my academic studies in Assyriology both conveniently and at a reasonable price. I came to rely on his catalogues to keep me abreast of what was being published in my field. It was likely soon thereafter that I first met him when he was manning the Eisenbrauns display table at an annual meeting of the American Oriental Society or the Rencontre Assyriologique Internationale. It was always a pleasure to go to the Eisenbrauns table since Jim was always friendly and genuinely interested in what one had to say. At least one stop at the Eisenbrauns display and a chat with Jim became an annual event. When I moved from the University of Toronto to the University of Pennsylvania in 2006 and created a new research project, the Royal Inscriptions of the Neo-Assyrian Period (RINAP), in order to finish the Assyrian side of the then-defunct Royal Inscriptions of Mesopotamia project (RIM), my first thought was to do it in connection with Eisenbrauns' publishing arm. Jim was immediately interested when I spoke to him about the matter and, after I explained the differences that I wanted to make to the RIM volumes and my plan to have online editions of the texts with Oracc (Open Richly Annotated Cuneiform Corpus), we quickly came to an agreement, one that I have never regretted. Once I had handed over a manuscript for my Royal Inscriptions of the Neo-Assyrian Period Project, Jim made sure that the book came out quickly and looked good. The fields of ancient Near Eastern studies and biblical studies owe Jim a tremendous debt for his herculean efforts in advancing our fields by facilitating access to publications from far-flung and, at times, obscure places and by producing a vast number of important publications at reasonable prices. *Multas gratias.*

SALLY MOREN FREEDMAN
Princeton University

JIM EISENBRAUN'S PERSONAL WARMTH AND ENTHUSIASM HELPED ME
to persevere in publishing research I began as a graduate student at the
University of Pennsylvania. The University Museum published volume
1 of the Babylonian omen series If A City Is Set on a Height in 1998
and volume 2 in 2006—though I wasn't involved in the publishing process at that point, I believe Eisenbraun's did the printing, and I know
they handled the books. Jim himself encouraged me to finish volume
3, which was published jointly by Eisenbrauns and the University of
Pennsylvania in 2017. In addition, he helped "recycle" a number of
books I had to sell, making it possible for these rare volumes to find
new homes with scholars who wanted them. After he gave up Eisenbrauns, he was most gracious in explaining that he was not able to help
bring volume 4 into print (which did not surprise me at all).

Jim's dedication to scholarly values is increasingly rare in a world
where commercial success seems to be the only goal publishers care to
pursue. He will be sorely missed, and the extraordinary contributions
he took the time and trouble to provide to the world's fund of knowledge and ideas will always be appreciated. Thank you, Jim!

LISBETH S. FRIED
University of Michigan

IT IS THRILLING TO WRITE A NOTE TO EXPRESS MY IMMENSE GRATI-
tude to Jim Eisenbraun and to all the folks at Eisenbrauns. Jim published
my first book, a revision of my doctoral dissertation at New York University. It is The Priest and the Great King: Temple-Palace Relations
in the Persian Empire (BJSUCSD 10; Winona Lake, IN: Eisenbrauns),
2004. Jim walked me through the whole process of turning a manuscript into a beautiful book. He was there to advise and to calm and
reassure me every step of the way, and he was a joy to work with.

Besides my book, Jim is to be warmly thanked, greatly appreciated,
and commended for the huge number of exceptional academic books
that he has published. These now grace my bookshelves. I was about to
count them, but they are countless, way beyond counting. It is because
of his own accomplishment as a scholar in his own right that he has
been able to select, edit, and publish such an outstanding collection.
By his own efforts he has furthered the whole field of biblical and near
eastern studies.

I also appreciate Jim for being a friendly and sociable presence at
the SBL and ASOR meetings. It is always a pleasure to see him and
his wife and have a friendly chat. I also appreciate all the great Eisenbrauns cups that grace my kitchen cabinet. Jim, may you go from
strength to strength.

ROY E. GANE
Andrews University

EACH NOVEMBER AT THE ANNUAL SBL BOOK DISPLAY IT WAS ESPE-
cially satisfying for me to see the long Eisenbrauns sign and Jim with
his long, wavy hair standing there chatting with some scholar while
his wife and others were selling books. This scenario conveyed the
impression that the biblical and ancient Near Eastern cosmic order
was continuing unabated. One day I was the scholar chatting with Jim
about the possibility of publishing a book. Jim was personable and open
to my proposal, even if the project would take several years, which it
did. Gerhard F. Hasel had told me that Eisenbrauns would be the best
publisher for my work, and I knew that he was right because Eisenbrauns delivered high quality in our field at reasonable prices. Jim set
a high standard through his personal involvement with the publishing
process, informed by his broad and deep knowledge and experience in
biblical and ancient Near Eastern studies, which he obviously loves. I
benefitted from his expertise and care when Eisenbrauns published my
book titled *Cult and Character* in 2005. I am deeply grateful to Jim and
his team for their excellent work. Eisenbrauns is continuing, thank-
fully, but I do miss the long sign, which I had thought would always be
there. May God be with our dear friend Jim as he moves into the future,
leaving all of us indebted to his monumental contribution.

AGNÈS GARCIA-VENTURA
Universitat Autònoma de Barcelona—IPOA, Universitat de Barcelona

I FIRST ATTENDED A *Rencontre Assyriologique Internationale* IN 2003. That year the event was celebrated in London (UK) and in the publishers' fair there was Jim Eisenbraun. Since then I met him several times at the *Rencontre*, but also at other meetings such as the annual one organised by the *American Schools of Oriental Research*. In all these meetings I visited Eisenbrauns' book stand, as it was a reference publisher.

In 2013 I co-organised, together with Saana Svärd, a workshop in the *Rencontre* held in Ghent (Belgium). Eisenbrauns was the publisher in charge of publishing these sessions held at the *Rencontre* as independent volumes, thus we approached him to talk about the future publication of our workshop. Since our first approach to Jim to discuss this issue, he was kind and easygoing. When we decided to include in the volume other chapters and to delay its publication, he was always flexible. The volume was finally out in 2018 under the title *Studying gender in the Ancient Near East*. This was the first edited volume I was working on, thus the experience gathered during this time was important for me from several points of view. Last but not least, I take advantage of this venue to thank Jim for his work and for the work of his team not only in this volume but also in the long list of volumes preceding this one, most of them reference ones in our field of study. Long life to Eisenbrauns' books!

W. RANDALL GARR
University of California, Santa Barbara

I MET JIM BEFORE 1980. HE WAS A BOOKSELLER AND SOLD BOOKS IN biblical and ancient Near Eastern topics, even from European presses. My customer ID number was 11121, so I thought he was very successful by the time I signed up. It seemed like he had a small operation, for whenever I ran into him (at a meeting) he was either alone or accompanied by his wife. Later that changed. He was, and remains, friendly and quite likeable.

I could not ask for a better publisher. Rumor has it that he typeset my first book in 1985 for the University of Pennsylvania Press. I hope that's true because the job was excellent. I know for a fact that he reprinted the same book later, at his own kind instigation. He send me a contract, I signed it, and not too much later I received a little box of reprinted books. Later, Steve Fassberg and I asked Jim if he would be interested in publishing a book we were organizing on the different forms of Biblical Hebrew. He was, and we remain grateful. It was not an ordinary typesetting job, either. He created a handful of symbols that I never saw elsewhere. We also had to pass through several versions of proofs, which he did without fuss. Throughout he was a mensch.

I am glad for Jim's success. I wish him כל טוב in the years to come. I sure hope he comes back for a meeting or two.

KRISTINE HENRIKSEN GARROWAY
Hebrew Union College

I WAS ONE OF MANY YOUNG SCHOLARS THAT WERE LUCKY ENOUGH TO have their first book published by Eisenbrauns. I could wax poetic about the feeling of elation I experienced when receiving the email accepting my manuscript, or the swell of emotion upon seeing my name on the spine of the completed book at the Eisenbrauns booth, but what I want to say most is, thank you, Jim. Thank you for changing my life forever, for making me a published author. Thank you for believing in me as you believed in so many others, for making the publishing process a positive one, for putting together an editorial team who pushed my ideas to make them better, and for running a press that published important works in a seemingly arcane field. Your vision and Eisenbrauns has left a mark on the field that will be hard to match. Whenever I look at a book carrying the ibex and Eisenbrauns name, it will bring a smile as I remember the man behind it all.

PETER J. GENTRY
University of Toronto

LOOKING BACK OVER MANY YEARS, I OWE A BIG DEBT TO JIM EISEN-braun—even though I certainly paid for all my books! It was during 1977–79, my Masters Degree in Near Eastern Studies at the University of Toronto, that I was driven to read and study the sources. As I searched for the sources and texts in the original languages, I quickly discovered two things: (1) the North American publishers like Baker, Eerdmans and Zondervan weren't supplying the fundamental sources, and (2) ordering these books from Europe was extremely difficulty and tricky and time consuming,not to mention downright expensive. Someone put me in touch with Eisenbrauns and I must say, I bought the majority of my scholarly tools from Jim's company.

I had no idea at the time of his labour and time, working out of his basement, to provide this marvelous service to scholars in North America. Without Eisenbrauns, I could never have put together the excellent reference library that is now my toolbox for research. And the mugs celebrating the ancient Near East supplied at SBL for big buyers like myself were an added bonus. Jim has also been a big friend to IOSCS, a society in which I have played a part. I am so thankful for JIm and his vision to help young scholars acquire the tools and it has been wonderful to get to know his family and staff at meetings like SBL. He has played an important part in my life since 1978.

SEYMOUR (SY) GITIN
W.F. Albright Institute of Archaeological Research, Jerusalem

I HAVE BEEN MOST FORTUNATE TO HAVE WORKED WITH JIM FOR THE past thirty years during which I have benefited greatly from his guidance and advice. He has been most generous with sharing his vast experience in editing and publishing, and I have always felt that he was committed to ensuring that whatever I was working on would be correctly published. Remarkable in his modesty and work ethic I hope that in his new arrangement with Penn State University Press that I will still have the opportunity of working with him.

ROBERT P. GORDON
University of Cambridge

JIM, NOT BEING A CONFERENCE JUNKIE, I HAVEN'T SEEN YOU AS OFTEN as some of our colleagues have over the years, and yet as I look at my bookshelves and my footnotes it seems that you are a daily presence here in the village of Comberton, five miles out of the older Cambridge. You have been a massive contributor in the world of Bible and ancient Near East for all these years, and a genial presence on all manner of occasions, valued and welcomed by colleagues even when they were not looking for a publishing outlet. You can rightly claim "Mission Accomplished" (the claim isn't always justified in operations connected with the Near and Middle East!). You have never lost the original vision of providing for student needs at student prices. You have set the bar high, and yet without bankrupting the young or old or their institutional libraries. And the publishing of fundamental and cutting edge work has prospered in your hand. No wonder Penn State welcomed you into the fold. It's reassuring that for another while there will still be the one shepherd guiding policy. I wish you many years of happy navigating. And may you find great satisfaction in fulfilling the role of honoured elder statesman among your grateful colleagues worldwide.

I have a particular memory that says a lot about you, and it relates to my time as editor of the *Vetus Testamentum* Book List. At one point it looked to you as if *VT* was excluding almost all your publications from the Book List, and you wrote such a gentle inquiry wondering whether this was policy or how it was happening. There was a complete absence of awkwardness or challenge about your inquiry, and I was delighted, after conducting some research, to be able to report that it was "the other publisher" that was failing to send review slips to Eisenbrauns, and that all your volumes were being noted, except in those cases where reviewers' eyes were bigger than their stomachs, and their ears deaf to entreaty. It was all so gracious of you, and of such is the kingdom of heaven!

ED GREENSTEIN
Bar-Ilan University

IT IS A CLICHÉ TO PRAISE A MAN AS A SCHOLAR AND A GENTLEMAN. But sometimes the phrase fits like a glove, or in Jim's case, like a dust cover. It is also a cliché to say that someone's name is synonymous with some cherished value. But it is nevertheless simple truth to say that the name of Eisenbrauns has been, and continues to be, synonymous with important and solid scholarship in the fields of ancient Near Eastern, biblical, and Semitics scholarship. And that is because Jim Eisenbraun is a scholar and, in the way he has built and run his business, a gentleman. He is as respected as the holder of a professorial chair. There may never have been anyone truly like him in the field.

I became acquainted with Jim when he first opened his typesetting, publishing, and book-selling business. I was an early client and supporter. For about thirty years, Eisenbrauns typeset and printed *The Journal of the Ancient Near Eastern Society*, a relationship that ended only with a hiatus in our publication and our turn to an exclusively online format. Jim and I have grown in the field in parallel, and for a long time our relationship was galvanized through our mutual friendship with the late great scholar, Michael Patrick O'Connor. I would always make a point of saying hi to Jim and to Myra at conferences and express my appreciation for all he has done and continues to do.

I can only wish Jim continued satisfaction in the first-rate and truly important work that he, Myra, and his team have done. It has always been an honor and pleasure to publish in an Eisenbrauns book; and I hope that I and many colleagues will continue to have that honor and pleasure for as many years as Jim and his team would like. Jim, you have been a great blessing to us. May you always be blessed.

STEVEN GROSBY
Clemson University

ABOUT TWENTY-FIVE YEARS AGO, I HAD A CONVERSATION WITH A professor of philosophy about my continuing and deepening interest in the religions and history of the ancient Near East. In hearing what I had to say, this unaccomplished yet overly confident, certainly self-inflated professor—characteristics typical of the majority of academics found throughout our institutions of higher education—responded, "Why would you want to be interested in that?"

That the humanities have come under criticism from pressures of vocational training for employment is well known. Those pressures are not new, as the existence of the American land grant universities attests; and perhaps those pressures are justified. Even so, one rarely finds historians of the ancient Near East in the departments of history in the vast majority of American universities that teach the country's future engineers, doctors, accountants, and lawyers. One learns to take for granted that the professors of those history departments know nothing about the three thousand year-long history of the ancient Near East, other than it has something to do with the Epic of Gilgamesh. But what was and remains dispiriting about that professor's response, and especially as it came from a professor of philosophy, is its dismissiveness of, even an assault upon, intellectual curiosity and the freedom of inquiry within the academy. This is the context for me not only to express my gratitude to, but also to praise, Jim Eisenbraun and his firm; for Eisenbrauns represented for me and many others an oasis, sustaining intellectual curiosity and serious inquiry, within this otherwise dreary state of affairs.

Eisenbrauns must have made a profit, as the firm existed for more than 40 years; but its published and impressively produced books were so affordable that I have wondered how it did. That the books published by Jim were so affordable meant that a scholar could have them in what, as a result, became a working, private library. Most, if not all, scholars working in the area of the ancient Near East have books published by Eisenbrauns in their personal libraries. I know that I have many. But as

Jim and Eisenbrauns are well known for having produced affordable and attractive books of serious scholarship devoted to the ancient Near East, I have wanted to emphasize in this appreciative tribute to Jim something beyond this obvious contribution. I want to emphasize his contribution to what is implied by the study of the history and religions of the ancient Near East: his contribution to the pursuit of intellectual curiosity, to the freedom of inquiry. By doing so, Jim made an important and necessary contribution to the continuation of our culture.

As the publisher of my *Biblical Ideas of Nationality: Ancient and Modern*, Jim supported me in the face of the dismissiveness of that Professor of Philosophy. I will forever be grateful to Jim for having done so, and especially as years ago I took up the then unfashionable investigation into the applicability of the category "nation" to the study of the ancient Near East. At that time, nationality was considered by many to be exclusively modern; but Jim was willing to entertain an argument that challenged the prevailing orthodoxy. Much has changed over the past twenty-five years. I still stand by the arguments of that initial exploration, but its publication gave me the confidence and opportunity to refine further that earlier and hesitant analysis by taking up investigations into the related conceptions of citizenship, boundaries, ethnicity, and states throughout the history of the ancient Near East. But that refinement would not have taken place if Jim had not provided me, as he did for many others, the support to pursue the problems aroused by curiosity, the very existence of which is made possible by the freedom of the mind.

MAYER I. GRUBER
Ben-Gurion University of the Negev

I HAD THE PLEASURE OF CONTRIBUTING TO THE FOLLOWING VOLUMES produced by Eisenbrauns: *Pomegranates and Golden Bells* (Jacob Milgrom Festschrift, 1995); *Birkat Shalom* (Shalom Paul Festschrift, 2008); *Mishneh Todah* (Jeff Tigay Festschrift, 2009); *From Author to Copyist* (Zipi Talshir Festschrift, 2015). I was privileged to be a coeditor and contributor to *Marbeh Hokhmah* (Victor Hurowitz Memorial Volume, 2015). It was always an honor and a pleasure to work with Jim Eisenbraun and his highly professional staff. He and his staff always went out of their way to work with authors and editors to produce flawless publications. Moreover, he remembered every face and name and publication as we passed in the hall at SBL Annual Meetings and other professional conferences.

ANSELM C. HAGEDORN
Universität Osnabrück

FOR AN UNDERGRADUATE IN BIBLICAL STUDIES IN EUROPE DURING THE
1990s the name Eisenbrauns almost had a mystical quality. A bookseller from a place in the United States I had never heard of that was
somehow able to procure all those books one would normally associate
with a university library. Of course, payment was always a problem—
but later an account with the Bayrische Hypothek- und Landesbank
made life much easier. A small letter including an invoice, bearing a
stylized ibex, printed with an old-fashioned needle printer was the first
harbinger of things to come. Much later (we were all saving on postage)
a sturdy box arrived with the desired book(s).

Little did I know, then, that there was much more to the name. This
changed, when my roommate in graduate school and I discussed our
reading list during the first week of the semester and he suggested that
we could just go to that "store" as a similar postcode suggested it just
being some miles away. 50 miles through amber waves of grain in rural
Indiana later, we were standing in front of a glorified shed and had a to
deal with a very puzzled receptionist who was clearly not used to walk-
in customers and announced, that she would call "Jim." For me, this
first encounter kind of epitomizes what makes Jim Eisenbraun who he
is. He displays an openness and genuine interest in anyone he meets. Of
course he took the time to show me around, tell me about Eisenbrauns
the publishing house and personally fetched what would become the
first of many Eisenbrauns books.

Many years later—and now a member of the editorial board of a
small monograph series published by Eisenbrauns—I came to realize
that the thing that makes Jim so special is a unique mixture of vision,
enabling possibilities and personal relationship without losing sight
of academic quality. Even after more than "40 years of good books"
he has never lost the vision how to do things differently. All the business is conducted with a unique personal touch—this can be a small
remark about inclement Indiana weather or a note on a bird Merna
and he spotted in their backyard. Our business meetings were much

more than business—easy and highly interesting conversations, never a dull moment and always conducted with good humour. I wish Merna and him all the best for retirement and hope they'll have time to read a book or two that is not in manuscript form.

GINA HANNAH
Eisenbrauns, Assistant to the President and Business Manager,
1998–2019

THOUGH I REALIZE THAT JIM MADE GREAT CONTRIBUTIONS TO
academia through his many years of building Eisenbrauns to a place of
prominence in the publishing world, my comments here will not focus
on that aspect of his life and career. I am not an academic—actually
more of a number nerd—and as Jim reaches this new chapter in his
life I find myself reflecting on the ways he impacted those of us who
worked alongside him through the years. That phrase, worked alongside, gives a hint to his style of leadership in the workplace. He took a
diverse group of individuals with a range of talents and strengths, not
to mention wildly different personalities, and created a collaborative
environment where everyone's voice was heard and each person was
released to do their best work without someone constantly leaning over
their shoulder. That style of leadership (not being the BOSS with a capital B all the time) comes with risk; and there were probably moments
when he doubted the wisdom of that approach; because mistakes were
made. Sometimes large-ish mistakes. In my 20 years, even I 😬 made
one or two that were memorable, but his response was always gracious,
the only requirement being that we all (including Jim) own our mistakes and learn from them.

It was impossible to work in close proximity with Jim and not learn
what was important to him outside of work. He deeply loves Merna
and his family; he has a passion for birdwatching, and when he is able
to enjoy good LIVE music he is in his happy place. Over the years I
also came to see that social justice was a big deal to him; caring about
and advocating for those that are often overlooked in our society was a
constant thread in his life and I am grateful for how that informed and
strengthened my own commitment to look outside my own interests
and pursue mercy and justice.

The last thing I want to mention about Jim is his great respect for
and empowerment of women. It probably helps that he is married to a
strong, confident woman! I feel a bit naive that until the recent #metoo

movement I really thought that treatment of women had greatly improved, especially in the workplace, but found it had only been pushed into dark corners and ignored. It was a gift to spend twenty years working in an environment where I never felt that my gender made me less than.

Thank you, Jim, for being both my employer and my friend! May you and Merna continue to find great joy and fulfillment in this next chapter.

G. GEOFFREY HARPER
Sydney Missionary and Bible College

AS I LOOK AROUND AT THE BOOKS ON MY OFFICE SHELVES, I AM reminded of the formative impact of Eisenbrauns volumes on my research and teaching. Many examples spring to mind.

My interest in intertextuality was piqued by Gordon Wenham's essay in *"I Studied Inscriptions from before the Flood": Ancient Near Eastern, Literary and Linguistic Approaches to Genesis 1–11* (Richard S. Hess and David T. Tsumura [eds.]; SBTS 4; 1994). Catherine McDowell's, *The Image of God in the Garden of Eden: The Creation of Humankind in Genesis 2:5–3:24 in Light of the mīs pî pīt pî and wpt-r Rituals of Mesopotamia and Ancient Egypt* (Siphrut 15; 2015), provoked substantial thinking with respect to what it means to be made in the image of God. Students have reaped the benefit of engaging with the nexus of biblical text and frontline archaeology through interaction with *"Did I Not Bring Israel Out of Egypt?": Biblical, Archaeological, and Egyptological Perspectives on the Exodus Narratives* (James K. Hoffmeier, Alan R. Millard, and Gary A. Rendsburg [eds.]; BBRSup 13; 2016).

What these volumes, and others, share is not merely a logo, but the ethos that Jim has instilled into each series and standalone book that Eisenbrauns has produced. His thoroughgoing commitment to present the best of biblical and ancient near eastern scholarship in an accessible format is everywhere apparent. Out of the many publisher booklists that cross my desk, Eisenbrauns consistently has something that I really must read.

Thank you, Jim, for not only crafting the vision but seeing it through. We stand in your debt.

GARY A. HERION
Hartwick College

THOSE OF US WHO TEACH RELIGIOUS STUDIES IN SMALL LIBERAL ARTS colleges know that we must often teach courses outside our area of specialized training. In my case, I had to develop a course on the historical Jesus. In the process I came across a photograph of Albert Schweitzer in his study jotting down notes for *The Quest of the Historical Jesus.* There sat Schweitzer at his desk, with stacks upon stacks of books piled up on the floor, with narrow paths between them so he could navigate his way around.

That reminded me of twenty years earlier, in 1976, when I was entering graduate school at The University of Michigan and going to buy my first books at Eisenbrauns. Jim and Merna lived in a trailer in Ann Arbor from which they sold hard-to-obtain books in ancient and biblical studies. They were wonderfully cordial when I dropped by their trailer that evening to buy copies of such things as Cyrus Gordon's *Ugaritic Textbook* and Wolfram von Soden's *Akkadisches Handwörterbuch.* There on the floor of their living space were stacks upon stacks of books. When I gave Jim my order, he snaked his way around the narrow paths to fill it. I was afraid to stray too far into the room for fear that I would disrupt whatever order he had imposed upon all those piles of books. And I remember thinking how fortunate I was that such an emporium of specialized books would be so easily available to we privileged few studying at The University of Michigan.

What a difference forty-three years has made. Today, all over the country—I dare say all over the world—people have felt fortunate to have that wonderful emporium of books that Eisenbrauns continues to offer, not just as a distributor but also now as a publisher. Each November at ASOR/SBL/AAR I would, like so many others, make a bee-line to the Eisenbrauns booth to see what Jim and Merna had on display.

Just last year, I had the pleasure for the first time of working with Jim as editor of a book that would bear the Eisenbrauns imprint. I felt truly honored to have that prestigious imprint (even if it was also shared with Penn State University Press). Jim was wonderfully supportive and generous throughout that process, just as he had been those many years earlier.

We are all so fortunate to have Jim, Merna, and Eisenbrauns on hand to enrich the work we do. I will always be grateful for that.

RICHARD S. HESS
Denver Seminary

JIM SEEMS TO HAVE ALWAYS BEEN THERE. FROM MY DAYS AS A SEMI-nary student in the late 1970s, when I first became acquainted with his listings of books for sale, until the present, Jim has consistently repre-sented the best in Bible and ancient Near Eastern studies and resources. His work as an editor and publisher has provided the highest quality in terms of content, style, and method. I came to respect his integrity and professionalism, knowing that what he published and the books he sold were at a fair and affordable price.

Getting to know Jim, whether as an author, an editor, or a customer, has been a privilege. He has always been the model of grace, friendship, and honesty. It was Jim who convinced me of the value of upgrading our *Bulletin for Biblical Research* journal from two to four issues a year, while we were in conversation over a cup of coffee in Leiden. Meet-ing him and Morna at professional meetings in the U.S.A. and around the world was one of the delights of those conferences. With them we shared something of our lives and families. Their presence at the Eisen-brauns book table will be greatly missed. May they know many more years of happiness and blessing.

JAMES K. HOFFMEIER
Trinity Evangelical Divinity School

JIM, CONGRATULATIONS ON AN ACCOMPLISHED CAREER IN PUBLISHING! Through Eisenbrauns publishing, you singlehandedly elevated the quality and quantity of Near Eastern publications in North America, placing Eisenbrauns on par with any European academic publishers, except that your monographs were affordable! Another indication of the caliber of material you have published over the years is that Penn State University Press will continue to publish using the Eisenbrauns brand. That is a tremendous achievement and will guarantee that your name will continue to be associated with high quality ancient Near Eastern publications.

I am a direct beneficiary of your professionalism. Your years of experience and eye for meticulous details in preparing manuscripts for publication was impressive. Now I know the when to use "mud brick" and mud-brick." Your passion to get things right and produce an excellent excavation report was impressive. *Tell el-Borg* I (2014) and II (2019) are a testimony to your excellent work. Thanks for helping me publish these volumes.

After decades of diligent work, I hope you enjoy your retirement and lots of wonderful time with your grandchildren!

TAWNY HOLM
The Pennsylvania State University

LONG BEFORE I KNEW JIM, I KNEW THE BOOKS—THE METICULOUSLY copyedited and typeset Eisenbrauns books—for whose catalog my colleagues and I eagerly awaited each season. All the best books in the field came from Eisenbrauns, a press lovingly and carefully run by Jim. I first met Jim himself at the book exhibit at an SBL conference, and it was even more of a pleasure to know the man himself. Jim is a consummate professional who is kind to everyone. Moreover, as the author of the first book in a new series he had conceived (Explorations in Ancient Near Eastern Civilizations), I can attest firsthand to Jim's courtesy and personal attention to every detail. Based on my own experience, I know he poured himself into every book that appeared in his press. Now, as an Eisenbrauns Editorial Committee member for Penn State University Press, I understand even better how much of Jim was invested in his company and in personal relationships with authors and the scholarly community. It is difficult to watch him retire, even though he deserves every moment of relaxation and ease after building a legacy in publishing excellence. I wish him well and will miss him personally and professionally.

JOHN HUEHNERGARD
The University of Texas at Austin

I DO NOT RECALL EXACTLY WHEN OR WHERE I FIRST MET JIM
Eisenbraun—it would of course have been at an AOS or SBL meeting—but I do recall knowing that I was meeting a celebrity. In the days
before the internet, I always rejoiced, like so many others, at the arrival
in the mail of the latest Eisenbrauns catalog or supplement. Not only
was this the easiest way to acquire a needed new book in the field; more
importantly, this was the best way simply to learn about the publication
of new books in the field, usually long before the first reviews would
appear in the journals. And then, with the field already greatly in his
debt, Jim made the risky decision to start publishing volumes himself.
And from the first volume, Waltke and O'Connor's indispensable and
now-standard *Introduction to Biblical Hebrew Syntax*, we knew that
a major publishing house had also arisen. The impact on our field
of Eisenbrauns as both publisher and distributor over the past four
decades cannot be overestimated.

My main professional association with Jim began when it was
decided that the various book series of the Harvard Semitic Museum
would be produced and distributed by Eisenbrauns. As a co-editor
of the Harvard Semitic Studies series, I was regularly in contact with
Jim about the process of publishing new volumes, the feasibility (or
desirability) of reprinting of volumes that had gone out of print, and
much more. In these matters Jim was invariably wise, knowledgable,
and accommodating — in short, a pleasure to work with. As an author
of books in the Harvard Semitic Series, too, I learned quickly to ask
for and rely on Jim's advice; the later editions of my *Grammar of Akkadian* and *Ugaritic Vocabulary* prominently mention my gratitude to
Jim for, quite simply, making the new editions possible in uncountable
ways. (They also mention his remarkable willingness, not conducive to
increased sales, to post the changes in the new editions on the Eisenbrauns website, so that owners of the earlier editions would not need to
buy the new ones.) The twenty-year partnership between the Harvard

Semitic Museum series and Eisenbrauns was wonderfully productive, and I cannot thank him enough for that.

Jim Eisenbraun is one of the first people I seek out at a conference. For the past decade or more, however, I have gone to the Eisenbrauns book table not to see what new volumes are on display, but to ask Jim what new birds Merna and he have seen. Since we discovered a shared love of birding, it has seemed entirely natural for reports of sightings of Snowy Owls or Caracaras to take precedence over news of the latest Eisenbrauns tomes. But eventually, of course, those bright new tomes do become too distracting to ignore — so many new books, in so many areas of our field!

Thank you, Jim, for "forty years of good books," and many years of friendship.

HERBERT B. HUFFMON
Drew Theological School

I FIRST MET JIM AND MERNA WHEN I VISITED THEIR TRAILER JUST outside Ann Arbor, over forty years ago. Jim was running a small book service out of one end of the trailer, supporting his graduate studies at the University of Michigan under George Mendenhall and David Noel Freedman. (His teacher at Grace Seminary, in Winona Lake, IND., was S. Herbert Bess, a Michigan graduate and the first doctoral student to finish under George Mendenhall.) Jim, having completed an M.A. and everything except his thesis, returned to Winona Lake, teaching at Grace Seminary from 1978–82.. He soon shifted his focus from teaching and selling books to publishing books. Academe may have lost a gifted teacher and scholar but it gained an extraordinary publisher. Indeed, as I have told Jim (and others) over the years, I am convinced that Jim as a publisher has contributed as much to biblical and ancient Near Eastern studies as any individual scholar presently in the field, and perhaps more.

Jim was born in China, doubtless of missionary parents, and he grew up in the upper peninsula of Michigan, a place known for independently minded people. Jim and Merna blazed their own path and Eisenbrauns has been on a long-term mission to the world of biblical and ancient Near Eastern scholarship. He is still at work. *Ad multos annos.*

CARMEN JOY IMES
Prairie College

JIM EISENBRAUN IS MORE THAN THE FOUNDER OF A PUBLISHING COM-
pany. He has been an enthusiastic encourager and friend to those who
have had the privilege of publishing with him. I first met Jim in 2013 at
SBL in Baltimore when it was my happy task to plan a celebratory dinner
for Dan Block coinciding with Eisenbrauns' publication of a Festschrift in
his honor. Jim was a distinguished guest. In a world where Festschriften
have no profit margin, Jim was one of the few publishers willing to facilitate the honor appropriate to the field -- in this case, for Dan Block's 40
years of teaching publishing in the area of Old Testament.

I was delighted when my dissertation was accepted for publication
in the Bulletin for Biblical Research Supplement Series, which meant
that it would bear the imprint of Jim's name. Mine was the first volume
in the BBRSup series to be published under the auspices of Penn State
University Press. I'm grateful that Jim remained involved during the
transition period to ensure its success. As a publishing house, Eisenbrauns has fostered and facilitated top quality academic work since
1975, longer than I've been alive. I continue to acquire helpful titles for
my personal library and to recommend them to my students.

Thanks, Jim, for your lifetime of effective service! You've made
a significant difference in the academy. Wishing you many long and
happy hours of reading and bird watching with Merna!

SHLOMO IZRE'EL
Tel-Aviv University

IT WAS SOMETIME DURING THE 1980S WHEN I FIRST MET JIM. IT WAS IN
a scholarly conference, where one of my colleagues introduced us to
each other. My recollection of this first meeting is that Jim was one
of the guys, taking part in the conference not as a publisher but as a
scholar. And indeed so it was and has been since: Jim is first and foremost a scholar. Yet, his contribution to the field is, of course, so much
broader and deeper that of what any single scholar could achieve in a
lifetime. Eisenbrauns has duly received its reputation as a core of scholarly education and research in the many related fields to the study of
the Bible and the ancient Near East.

Coming myself from a family of publishers, I can really appreciate
the kind of publisher Jim is: striving for publishing good, worthy books
rather than aiming at publishing books just for the sake of publishing
or aiming to achieve wider distribution. This has also been my own
experience with all my interactions with Jim throughout the years, as
an author, as an editor and as a reviewer. The amount of work invested
in each of the publications is worthy of admiration and respect. Jim
really cares!

Jim indeed deserves our deep gratitude for his contribution to our
diverse fields of interest and research, but first and foremost for who he
is: a kind, caring and wonderful human being. A big Thank You, Jim!

ETHAN C. JONES
Southwestern Baptist Theological Seminary

SO FAR AS I KNOW, THERE IS NO CLASS OR SEMINAR ON HOW TO PUT together an edited volume from start to finish (at least that would translate to the field of ancient Hebrew). Several years ago I knew the authors and ideas I wanted in the book. I also knew (however naively) that it would serve the field of Hebrew studies. Beyond that, I had nothing. Of course, I had various skills that would help, but there was no blueprint for how the process of publishing an edited volume (with all its complexities) was supposed to work.

Then enter Jim. Upon accepting my proposal, he took this young scholar and helped me understand how it all worked. He did not mince words on the difficulties of keeping scholars on task. Holding Hebraists to deadlines is far from easy, he would explain. And so it was. Yet with his guidance and sage advice, I learned to (gently) update and often remind the authors of where our progress should be.

Jim was always quick to encourage, educate, and simply help. Over the course of putting the book together, he received and answered more than a few emails. His messages would always be clear, succinct, and seasoned with kindness. I would never walk away confused about what he meant or what I should do next. His leadership (and the team around him) helped bring my idea into published form.

Thanks to Jim, I learned much about the details of editing and (more importantly) how to navigate the human element of scholarship—attitudes, preferences, and the inevitable delinquent contributor not excluded. My experience with Jim gave me a clear picture of excellence—both professionally and personally—in the world of academic publishing. I will be forever grateful for the opportunity to have worked with him, especially as he was well seasoned in his career and I being nothing if not green. To him, however insufficient it may be, I would like to say "Thank you."

CHARLES E. JONES
The Pennsylvania State University Library

IT IS A GREAT PLEASURE TO JOIN WITH SO MANY OF HIS FRIENDS IN THIS
tribute to Jim, a truly monumental figure in ancient Near Eastern
and biblical studies. Jim and his firm have been a huge presence for
the entirety of my professional life. His dedication to truly enduring
scholarship and his deep sense of responsibility to his authors, editors,
readers, and customers is legendary. It is hard to imagine the many professional and learned society meetings he attended without his smiling
and friendly presence. He always seemed to be everywhere. In recent
years Eisenbrauns presence in the lives of his customers through email
and social media has been constant without ever being intrusive.

I vividly remember the first time I met Jim. I can't pin down the
date precisely, but it was shortly after I commenced my position as
Librarian at the Oriental Institute Research Archives, and after the
arrival at the Oriental Institute of Tom Holland, hired to be the Head
of a newly revived in-house publication program. Jim was in Chicago
meeting with Tom to discuss the distribution and sale of Oriental Institute books. Tom called my office and asked if I would like to meet Jim.
I jumped at the chance and the two of them walked down to my office
where we had a conversation about books and publishing and library
collections. Despite the fact the this was thirty-five years ago I vividly
remember the sense that I was rude to him in being critical of some
delays in delivery of books he was selling from a third party. These
delays were of course entirely out of his control. He characteristically
showed no visible offence at my naïve and untoward words, apologized,
and assured me he would work to fix the problem. And he did. I doubt
that Jim remembers this exchange, but in any case, I take this opportunity to apologize on behalf of my rash and youthful self and thank Jim
for his gentlemanly response.

Nearly a quarter century later, when I was Head Librarian at the
still new Institute for the Study of the Ancient World at New York
University working on the next phase of a career-long interest of mine

in providing digital access, free of charge to the user, to high quality scholarship on the ancient world. I approached Jim and asked for a few moments of his time to pitch a proposal. We met in the hotel lobby and found a reasonably quiet corner and settled into comfortable chairs. We chatted about this and that, mutual friends, the book trade, library purchasing trends and so on. Eventually I got to the point and asked him (as I had done with other publishers) if he would be willing to make any of his out of print back-list openly and globally accessible in the HathiTrust Digital Library. His response was immediate: "Chuck, Eisenbrauns books do not go out of print"! He then explained his practice of publishing scholarship of enduring value without a sell-by date and to assure its availability to his customers at fair and reasonable prices. It was an astonishing thing to hear and seemed to perfectly encapsulate Jim's philosophy.

Most recently is has been a great privilege to play a small role in the successful transition of Eisenbrauns into an imprint of the Penn State University Press. For some years I had been aware of Jim's desire to develop a succession plan for his firm which would allow him to retire. It was clear that he wished Eisenbrauns to continue its traditions of excellent scholarship and service to authors, editors, readers, and customers. It was also clear that he did not wish to take the easy (and probably lucrative) path and sell to one or another of the rapaciously acquisitive publishing giants that so dominate the book making landscape of the twenty-first century. Though I did not know details, I was aware of some of the attempts he was making to ensure a transition and the problems he was encountering. Not long after my move to Penn State University Library I was invited to be a member of the Penn State University Press Editorial Committee. Eventually Patrick Alexander, the Director of the Press, engaged me in conversations in strictest confidence, about his negotiations with Jim. Needless to say, I was an enthusiastic supporter of the idea. Patrick filled me in from time to time of the progress of the talks, and eventually asked me to play a role in making a convincing argument to the Penn State Dean of University Libraries and Scholarly Communications, the unit of this University in which the Press sits., and who is my boss. We were evidently successful and following a formal agreement Eisenbrauns began to be integrated as a part of PSU Press. It was not a simple transition, but Patrick Alexander and his colleagues at the Press worked diligently and from, my perspective at least, it appears now to be a success. Jim continued his role as acquisitions editor during the transition and during this period I had the opportunity of a window into Jim's editorial practice. This came in the form of establishing an Editorial Committee for the Eisenbrauns imprint. Patrick Alexander asked me to recommend members of the Penn State University faculty to serve on the Board. We discussed some possible names, and Patrick eventually invited Tawny Holm, Michael Legaspi, and me to serve. We have met several times and reviewed and discussed many manuscripts often offering suggestions for improvement or clarification and discussing potential use of the books, and its markets. Most interesting in this transitional period was that it offered us and members of the editorial staff of the Press to hear Jim talk about his practices and to ask him to clarify how he has operated in the past. I believe he learned a lot about the way the Press operates, and I know we were lucky to have his learned and experienced voice in the room. As the date of Jim's retirement approached, the Press advertised and selected a short list of candidates for the position of Acquisitions Editor for the Press's Eisenbrauns imprint. We member rof the Editorial Committee were invited to interview the candidates and to offer our opinions. A very excellent successor was appointed. Jennifer Singletary begins here in State College on the very day I write this.

In the meantime, Jim formally began his long-awaited retirement. He and Merna are now free to travel and enjoy themselves without the tether of email and responsibility to their firm. I wish them well in their future and look forward to seeing them again soon!

JIM KINNEY
Baker Publishing Group

I AM PLEASED TO OFFER A FEW WORDS IN HONOR OF JIM EISENBRAUN and his contribution to the academy. I have no shortage of good things to say about Jim, but I have found this tribute difficult to write. Anything I say will fall far short of expressing the impact Jim has had on my life both personally and professionally, and the depth of my gratitude to him. On the other hand, if I tried to express that gratitude more fully, this piece would quickly become too personal for a public setting. With those limitations in mind, I nonetheless press on.

I met Jim Eisenbraun in September of 1988. My wife Linda and I had recently moved to Winona Lake, Indiana, where I planned to attend seminary while working full time. Linda had taken a job at Eisenbrauns earlier in the summer. When a shipping position came open, she helped connect me with the opportunity.

The business was small at that time—about twenty employees. Even though Jim was the owner, all of us saw him in action every day and got to know him pretty well. He was the first scholar I had ever been around for an extended period of time. Having moved to Winona Lake from a fundamentalist Baptist church, I didn't know what to do with either Jim or the business; Jim didn't fit neatly into any of my preconceived categories. But there was something about him that intrigued me, kept me coming back to work each day, and eventually led to my personal and professional transformation.

It was easy to see that Jim is an incredibly gifted and talented individual. Running a small business requires any number of skills and competencies: finance, technology, physical plant, personnel, logistics, and so on. Jim had built Eisenbrauns from scratch and so had all of those competencies. He could reprogram the computer, fix the truck, file taxes, and everything else. But he could also edit and typeset the most difficult books one could imagine: illustrated archeological reports, transcriptions of ancient cuneiform texts, studies in Hebrew linguistics, and more. Oh, and he was also overseeing a catalog bookseller, selling specialist resources to Assyriologists, archeologists, and biblical scholars around the world. My first reaction to Jim, then, was to marvel at the array of talents he possessed.

As the business grew, Jim was able to delegate many of these tasks to others. And that growth and expansion showed another set of Jim's talents. His genuine concern for people came through in his dealings with others, whether inside the business or outside. It's not that everything was perfect or idyllic. In any business, as with any human endeavor, plenty goes wrong. But Jim offered us the unique combination of non-anxious presence, eternal optimist, humanitarian realist, entrepreneurial pragmatist, and considerate caregiver.

Perhaps the most important thing for me to note about Jim is his integrity. I saw Jim interact with his wife and children, with his employees, with authors, with vendors, and even with a local church where we served on a leadership board together for a time. He was the same person in each of those contexts. He wasn't always right. Nor did he always live up to his own high standards. But he was consistent in providing oversight, wisdom, and care. If something went wrong, he would work to make it right. If he took a misstep, he would correct it and move on. And he would call those around him to do the same: to pursue excellence, honesty, and compassion.

After eight years at Eisenbrauns, I took a position with another publisher, where I've now been for twenty-three years. But Eisenbrauns did more than help me discover my career path. The culture of the business gave me a model for how smart people can work together with passion, skill, respect, and candor. Hard work can be immensely satisfying in such an environment. My time with Jim also offered me fundamental ideas and ideals about editorial and book production values, author care, and the business of publishing. After thirty years of publishing, it's hard for me to unravel where certain ideas and approaches have come from. But I think of everything I do now as being informed by or a logical extension of the foundation that was laid for me at Eisenbrauns many years ago.

More than all of the above, Jim and Merna helped Linda and me in our personal lives in incalculable ways. They showed us a way of living together as a couple and as a family with mutuality, openness, courage, and tenderness. Without saying more than that, I'll simply say thank you to them both.

Jim Eisenbraun, through the business that he started on a shoestring back in 1975, has left an indelible mark on the academic publishing world. In the early days he provided resources to scholars and reprinted some classic works that still help form young scholars. As the business grew, Jim distributed books for a variety of scholarly publishers and societies who needed the help of a skilled bookseller. He also provided typesetting services to journals and book publishers who needed his language and font expertise. With Michael O'Connor's *Hebrew Verse Structure,* Jim began publishing original works in 1980. And now, forty-five years after those humble beginnings, he has published hundreds of indispensible resources for scholars and students. The little ibex logo on the spine of Eisenbrauns books says something about their quality, their curation, and their significance.

With the Eisenbrauns torch now passed to Penn State University Press, it is time for Jim to enjoy a retirement that I hope includes much time to reflect on a lifetime spent serving the academy. Jim worked incredibly hard for many years out of a love of humanity, a quest for knowledge and understanding, and a devotion to service. I'm pleased to add my voice to the chorus of those expressing to him our gratitude for his dedication and accomplishments.

GERALD A. KLINGBEIL
Andrews University

"BLESSED IS HE WHO READS…" (REV 1:3):
TRACING INTERSECTING LIFE JOURNEYS

I FIRST MET JIM EISENBRAUNS MORE THAN 20 YEARS AGO DURING THE
1999 Midwest regional meetings of the American Schools of Oriental
Research, the American Oriental Society, and the Society of Biblical
Literature. This was the second international scholarly meeting that I
was able to attend. At that time, I was teaching at Universidad Peruana
Union, close to Lima, Peru, and funding for participation in international scholarly meetings was not easy to come by.

Jim awed me. During my postgraduate studies I had always appreciated the quality books published by Eisenbrauns and felt encouraged
by their "reasonable" pricing. I spent a lot of time around the small
exhibit table offering Eisenbrauns books and other volumes focusing
on the ancient Near East at that meeting at HUC. I was also intrigued
to see Jim sit in many sessions that were relevant to Eisenbrauns' publishing focus. Usually he was just an engaged listener, though I saw him
speaking to presenters one on one following these sessions.

During my postgraduate studies at Stellenbosch University in South
Africa and completion of a D.Litt. in Ancient Near Eastern Studies in
1995, it had been well nigh impossible to travel to international meetings. That is why my first North American academic meetings were
highly significant. I still remember the wonder I felt when I entered
the book exhibit of the SBL Annual Meeting and saw the quantity of
academic volumes that I had only known from the library at Stellenbosch. I saw Jim at most of these meetings, and we spoke briefly at
some of them, but I imagine he would not even remember these occasions. Jim spoke to a lot of people, and even more people knew him.
This young German (where I was born and raised) scholar working in
South America would not have caught his attention as he was always
scanning the crowd for current and potential Eisenbrauns authors. I

surely never imagined that one day I would also belong to this "illustrious" group of people.

After moving to Argentina in December 2000 to teach at Universidad Adventista del Plata, I started to make plans for a monograph focusing on reading biblical ritual texts and brought a proposal to the next annual meeting a year later. Since I had not studied at a North American university, American publishers seemed to be more hesitant to publish research from scholars who did not have a "known" pedigree. Additionally, many publishers focusing on biblical studies had begun to move away from academic monographs and were embracing more whole-heartedly the production of textbooks that offered a larger sale market. During this time I also met Rick Hess, who had recently become editor of the *Bulletin for Biblical Research*, an academic journal published by the Institute for Biblical Research and Eisenbrauns. By now I had a completed manuscript in hand and after reading it and sending it out for peer review, it was recommended for publication as the inaugural volume of the newly established Bulletin for Biblical Research Supplement series. I was delighted. The next year was filled with annotated chapters of the book moving between Libertador San Martín, Argentina; Denver, Colorado; and Winona Lake, Indiana. I remember reading the final proofs of my volume during a week spent in South Korea on a teaching assignment, marveling at the elegant layout and the extraordinary carefulness and skill of the Eisenbrauns editorial staff. As a detail person I really like accurate footnotes, but these people were more "obsessed" than I was! It's a blessing to have competent and engaged editors.

I had become part of the large family of Eisenbrauns authors—and was proud of it. During the 2007 SBL annual meeting in San Diego my volume was discussed in a review session by a group of scholars working in the field of ritual studies. I particularly cherished the presence of Ron Grimes, the eminent pioneer of ritual studies within the context of religious studies. Naturally, Jim sat in the back of the session room and, in his quiet ways, offered a genuine congratulation.

A year later I was privileged to coedit together with Rick Hess and Paul Ray Jr. another volume in the Bulletin for Biblical Research

Supplement series focusing on ancient Israelite history. By then I had realized that royalties in academic publishing were a subliminal means of publishers to induce more shopping for I am sure that I have spent more on Eisenbrauns volumes that I ever received in royalties.

Let me conclude this brief reflection on my personal journey intersecting with Jim Eisenbrauns' journey with a reference to the introduction of the New Testament book of Revelation: "Blessed is he who reads..." (Rev 1:3). Jim has most likely read thousands of manuscripts. Some were brilliant; others didn't make the cut. In each case he graciously shared of his wisdom, his passion for biblical and ancient Near Eastern studies, and his expertise in academic publishing. I am grateful for his ability to look beyond academic pedigrees to content, for reading surely is the beginning of understanding and understanding is always an invitation to grow and become a blessing to those around us. Jim and his team have been a blessing to me. May his tribe increase and may Eisenbrauns (even as an imprint of Penn State University Press) never grow weary of publishing focused monographs and reference works dealing with the fascinating world of the Bible and the ancient Near East.

ANDREW KNAPP
Eerdmans
Eisenbrauns Acquisitions Editor and Marketing Manager, 2012–2015

OTHER CONTRIBUTORS TO THIS VOLUME WILL UNDOUBTEDLY FOCUS on the impact that Eisenbrauns has made on the field, and justly so. With seminal books such as Waltke and O'Connor's *Introduction to Biblical Hebrew Syntax* and flagship series such as Mesopotamian Civilizations and Languages of the Ancient Near East, Eisenbrauns has made an imprint on all scholars of the Hebrew Bible and the ancient Near East in the last half century. I can't count the times I have typed "Winona Lake, IN" into a bibliography, and there are many who have done so far more often than I. But as one of the few who admires Jim not only for his publishing legacy but also for his work as an employer, I will focus on the latter in this tribute.

I have cherished Eisenbrauns for as long as I have been in the field. Their location at the intersection of ancient Near Eastern and biblical studies coincides with mine, and their commitment to producing high-quality books—both in content and production—at prices that allow individuals to purchase them is laudable, especially given the model of most of their peers in academic publishing. So I always daydreamed of publishing a book with Rex the ibex on the spine.

But life contains many unexpected twists. Rather than looking to Winona Lake to help me rear my literary offspring, I found myself raising my biological offspring in the lovely hamlet of north-central Indiana. Eisenbrauns advertised an acquisitions editor opening during my final year of graduate school; I applied and was invited for an on-campus (so to speak) interview. My wife, Kandace, and I arrived in Winona Lake apprehensively—while excited by the prospect of joining Eisenbrauns, like most other starry-eyed young biblical scholars I had expected to take a university job in which I would produce articles that would revolutionize the field while molding minds and changing lives in the classroom. And having absquatulated from South Bend just five years before, we never anticipated putting down roots in the Hoosier State again. But the job, the area, and Jim and Merna won us over rapidly. The point of no return came in my first conversation with Jim, during which I discovered that some years before, to celebrate his birthday, he and Merna had managed to get the Vigilantes of Love to perform in downtown Warsaw. I had found a kindred spirit.

I spent two and a half pleasant years at Eisenbrauns, traversing the Winona Lake Trails then hugging the beautiful, eponymous lake to get to the office each day. Our son entered the world in Kosciusko Community Hospital, and our daughter transformed from a baby to a big kid. Throughout this time, as I struggled to keep up with the pressures of a young family and a new job, Jim worked tirelessly to maintain Eisenbrauns's sterling reputation and secure its future. I absorbed so much from Jim during this apprenticeship—about the publishing industry, about the field and its many fascinating denizens, about editing, about professionalism, about adapting to changes in an unstable business environment. Jim demonstrated unlimited patience and generous hospitality through it all.

When it became probable that the future of Eisenbrauns most likely would not include me, we reluctantly uprooted the family and headed north to Michigan. What I learned from Jim has enabled me to have success in my new publishing venture, and I remain grateful for my time with Eisenbrauns. As the company enters its next phase of life, without the force of nature who founded and guided it for more than forty years, I pray that those now leading the company will solidify its place in the field and reputation for generations to come, as befits Jim's legacy. Thank you, Jim, for what you've done for me and for the field. Long live Rex!

JOHN F. KUTSKO
Society of Biblical Literature

IN THE WALLS OF URUK HE INSCRIBED UPON A STONE

THE FIELDS OF BIBLICAL AND ANCIENT NEAR EASTERN STUDIES OWE A
debt to Jim Eisenbraun. He helped them thrive because of his personal
commitment and even sacrifice, because publishing was his scholarship, because of the scholarship he published, because of many tenure
and promotions granted through his high standards of publishing, and
because of the careers he inspired in publishing itself. Many tributes
have focused on Jim and his dedication to authors, editors, and his
beloved Eisenbrauns—the scholarship and the scholars he supported.

However, the model he set for many, including me, also deserves
mention. Jim paved the way for scholars to choose editing and publishing, and inspired the careers of many. It is no small coincidence
that he studied under the quintessential editor of our field, David Noel
Freedman. Noel Freedman's commitment to publishing as a scholarly
vocation was palpable in the offices of the Program on Studies in Religion at the University of Michigan. One couldn't help but catch the
bug. At a time when anything less than the professoriate was second-
class, Noel signaled how great an art and science editing and publishing
were. Jim is proof of that—of the grand vocation of scholarly publishing by scholars themselves.

Two things strike me about Jim, the legacy of his imprint, and his
vocation making books written by others that unquestionably have his
fingerprints on them. Jim reminds me of Robertson Davies' novel *The
Fifth Business*. The title refers to the character in a drama or opera who
is not the protagonist or villain, hero or heroine, but who nevertheless is essential in bringing about the denouement and meaning of the
story. Jim and Eisenbrauns was the fifth business, not merely a publishing business.

One of the greatest epics of his beloved field, ancient Near Eastern
studies, has an image that also reminds me of Jim and Eisenbrauns. The
prologue of the Epic of Gilgamesh, added later, establishes the meaning

of the story as story. The permanence of the story and its hero are in print and in stone. Immortality is not in the adventure (though there was adventure for Jim), but in writing it down, in the tablet on which it is written, in the box in which it is stored, and upon the shelf upon which it is set, an insight into Gilgamesh that comes from an author Jim published.* The unpublished adventure fades in memory. Its record makes it immortal. Jim's epic, now immortal, is inscribed on tablets of lapis lazuli, set in boxes of copper, and deposited in the walls of Uruk.

* Piotr Michalowski, "Sailing to Babylon, Reading the Dark Side of the Moon." Pp. 177–94 in *The Study of the Ancient Near East in the 21st Century: Proceedings of the Albright Centennial Symposium*. Edited by Jerrold S. Cooper and Glenn M. Schwartz. Winona Lake, IN: Eisenbrauns, 1996. See pp. 188–89.

BERNARD M. LEVINSON
University of Minnestoa

AMID THE SHOCK OF FLOWING HAIR AND LONG BEARD: A FRIEND AND
colleague, never simply a publisher. Jim has always been there, directly
or indirectly, for the entire period of my academic career, ever since I
began graduate school in the last century and in the last millennium.
Although these memories of origins are not quite antediluvian, they
do seem in their own way primordial. I first learned of Jim Eisenbraun
in 1977 during my first semester in graduate school, at McMaster University in Hamilton, Ontario, where I was fortunate to have had Alan
Cooper as my first real teacher of Hebrew Bible, where he had begun
his own academic career as a faculty member just the year before. We
had a seminar on Job and he told the class about a then new mailorder
bookstore specific to Hebrew Bible and ancient Near East, run by a
graduate student, seeking to sell books as economically as possible.
Several of us pooled resources for the cross-border purchase, which
was then my first real academic book order period. That was Jim, then
in Ann Arbor; he and Merna were there from 1974 through 1978; and
then moved to the famed Winona Lake, Indiana, location in mid-1978,
after courses and comps.

   I didn't meet him directly of course until much later. The first real
working project was the volume that Gary Knoppers (who is much
missed) and I collaborated on, which arose out of a series of sessions at
the International Society of Biblical Literature meeting in Edinburgh,
which became *The Pentateuch as Torah: New Models for Understanding Its Promulgation and Acceptance* (2007). Gary had previous worked
with Jim on several other edited volumes. With this project, there was
a real sense of team work: between Gary and me as editors, but equally
with Jim and his staff (Bev McKoy, James Spinti, Andrew Knapp, Andy
Kerr, Gina Hannah), who were a pleasure to work with. They were
invested in quality writing and editing, sensitive to academic politics,
committed to creative cover design, and had a broader sense of academic values. It took a lot of work but the volume was successful and, I
believe, continues to provide a resource to the field.

More than many publishers, Jim has a clear vision of supporting both readers and authors, He makes a point of attending all the major international conferences to showcase the multiple titles he published, and did so in multiple fields, both biblical studies and Assyriology. He equally warehoused otherwise difficult to access foreign publications and established formal distribution relationships for series like the State Archives of Assyria, Ugarit Forschungen, and the multiple series of Mohr Siebeck. Jim also generously would provide a resource as someone to consult even for advice about what to look for (and what to avoid!) in contracts with other publishersIt was consequently an honor to be invited to help launch a new monograph series published by Eisenbrauns, Critical Studies in the Hebrew Bible. The invitation came from its very engaged editors, Anselm Hagedorn and Nathan MacDonald. Striking was the vision of (mercifully) short monographs to serve a specific need. Equally striking was the commitment of Jim and his team to do the best possible job of copyediting and production: that the editors (Bev!) really knows both writing and academic content, knew the conventions of the field, was someone you could trust (which is not always the case these days with even the fanciest university presses who outsource their copyediting and production). Here even when the page proof PDF files had to go back and forth multiple times to get the layout of complicated appendices or indexes correct, they were committed to getting it right.

That is what Jim and Merna helped give birth to: a publisher committed to getting it right, where the working relationship was closer to being colleagues, where there was a real human being at the other end, and a friend.

JOEL N. LOHR
Hartford Seminary

IT'S HARD TO EXPRESS THE SENSE OF EXCITEMENT AND FULFILLMENT that comes with publishing that first book. Eisenbrauns did that for me, and Jim Eisenbraun, even though he was the highest-ranking figure at the press, guided me through the process every step of the way. He answered my every question, helped me understand a whole new world, and there are things about that process, and the way Eisenbrauns edited my monograph, that have stayed with me ever since, making me a better writer and editor.

What I appreciate most about Jim is his complete lack of academic stuffiness or pretentiousness. I come from a construction background, in fact a long line of carpenters, and Jim made me feel completely at home. He broke down barriers for me at a time when I needed it. When I finally got to meet Jim in person, at an SBL conference, he was everything I had expected, and more. Warm, welcoming, and accepting, with a beard of biblical proportions—for which he is known. Congratulations, Jim, on a hugely successful career, for furthering the field of ancient Near Eastern and biblical studies, but most importantly for bringing a human touch to our field.

TREMPER LONGMAN III
Westmont College

BIBLICAL AND ANCIENT NEAR EASTERN STUDIES OWES AN IMMENSE debt of gratitude to Jim Eisenbrauns for his tireless and joyful work in support of our research for over four decades. I remember entering the field in the late 1970s and discovering the Eisenbrauns book catalogue as the place to buy the best books in the field for the most reasonable price. Later, when it came time to seek a publisher for my dissertation in the early 1990s, Eisenbrauns was my first choice not only because of the high quality of their books, but also because they sold their books at a reasonable price. In more recent years, I have worked with Jim as one of the editors of the prestigious series Siphrut and along with my colleagues (Stephen Chapman and Nathan MacDonald) have found his passion to be contagious and his insightful guidance invaluable. Jim, however, was not only my publisher, he became my friend as he has many others in our field. I have (and still do) relish not only our email exchanges but also the times we get to talk at SBL. And, as we honor Jim, we should never forget Merna, who also has dedicated her efforts to publish the best that our fields have to offer. Thank you, Jim and Merna!

NATHAN MACDONALD
University of Cambridge

I WANT TO OFFER TWO STORIES ABOUT JIM. ONE FROM EARLY IN THE time I got to know him, and one more recent. The first story concerns the origins of the Critical Studies in Hebrew Bible. I'd got to know Jim when Tremper Longman and Stephen Chapman proposed my name as a third editor of the Siphrut monograph series. It was perhaps a year later at an SBL meeting at Atlanta that I had one of those late-night conversations with another publisher and Stuart Weeks from Durham about an essay that I had written that had far outgrown the length that a journal would accept, but was still too short to make a decent length book. As I recall, Stuart met my lamentations with a shrug of the shoulder. I wasn't the first academic to be in this dilemma. Pop in the drawer and return to in the future and perhaps you'll have further insight about what to do with it. I turned to the publisher and complained that we needed a series for short books, after all weren't many of the great classic works such as Noth's *Deuteronomistic History* actually quite short, and many monograph series such as the JSOTSup and Studies in Biblical Theology begun with quite short and focussed studies. But the publisher couldn't see it working. It didn't fit the models that the publishing industry had developed.

I already knew enough about Jim to know if anyone could make the idea work it would be him. He knew his business from top to bottom, the costs and the margins, and the market. So the following morning I pitched the idea to him: a short monograph series, affordable, in paperback, focussed studies by established scholars that other scholars would want on their shelves. What I did not appreciate then, but did soon afterwards, was that Jim not only knew his business, but even forty years in, he still had the vision about how to do things differently. After that conversation, an idea that was unworkable with another publisher the night before was well on the way to becoming a reality.

My other story is more recent and describes another aspect of Jim—and Merna. I arrived at my B&B for the recent IOSOT conference in Aberdeen to discover that I was not the only IOSOT attendee staying. Purely by chance, my fellow editor Anselm Hagedorn as well as Jim and Merna had booked into the same B&B. We met every morning for breakfast which became rather lengthy affairs. We had already arranged to have dinner together and we kept the appointment despite the fact that we had no business to conduct that we hadn't already covered over breakfast. And why not? Jim and Merna are easy company and the conversation flows seamlessly from life in Warsaw, Indiana, through the scholars of the past and the present, trends in the field, American and European politics. Never dull, never unreflective, and always full of a gentle and generous humour.

Jim and Merna, enjoy your retirement, and may every day begin with an unrushed breakfast.

PETER MACHINIST
Harvard University

JIM EISENBRAUN IS AND WILL ALWAYS REMAIN FOR ME THE MODEL OF the scholar publisher, a combination rarely found, let alone matched. I have followed with admiration the development of his firm, Eisenbrauns, from tentative, modest bookselling to publishing, becoming in the process one of the really major academic centers for the fields of biblical and ancient Near Eastern studies. The quality of Eisenbrauns' publications has always been at the highest level: meticulous copyediting, elegant fonts and formats for all the relevant scripts and languages, attractive, even stunning covers, and accessible pricing.

Exemplary in this regard is the way in which Jim took over the complexities of the *CAD*, continuing, indeed improving on the work of its previous publisher, despite the initial doubts of the *CAD* editors. Equal results I was honored to receive personally in the Festschrift volume for me whose publication by Eisenbrauns Jim so capably supervised. Throughout Jim has been a deep and gracious friend and advisor to all with whom he has worked. I count myself very lucky to have been one of the many beneficiaries of his outstanding success.

Jim—*mazal tov; ad multos annos!*

MADABA PLAINS PROJECT-ʿUMAYRI

Douglas Clark (La Sierra University), Larry Herr (Burman University), Lawrence Geraty (La Sierra University), and Monique Vincent (Walla Walla University)

IT HAS BEEN AN ABSOLUTE PRIVILEGE AND PLEASURE ENCOUNTERING and engaging Jim Eisenbraun at conferences like SBL and ASOR over the past four decades. Few publishers hovering over booksellers' tables are as recognizable, as affable, as approachable, as knowledgeable as Jim. They don't come any better. Nor do publishers come much better. Eisenbrauns has set and held to high standards of scholarship, ethical principles, generous business communications, timely release schedules, and stellar publication quality and aesthetic presentation.

For these reasons, directors of the Madaba Plains Project excavations at Tall al-ʿUmayri, Jordan approached Jim about publishing its seasonal volumes. Actually, approached him a number of times over several years when previous publication arrangements stalled. If patience is a virtue, Jim is a virtuous man, having endured annual-meeting conversation after annual-meeting conversation about our publication needs. Finally, we made the shift to Eisenbrauns in the publication of the ʿUmayri seasonal reports—volumes 7 (the 2000 season) and 8 (2002 season). We have submitted volume 9 (2004 season) with volume 10 (2006 season) on the way and the remainder to follow. We look forward to continuing the series through the 2016 season, now likely the final one at ʿUmayri due to ongoing disputes between land owners and the government of Jordan.

Three things have made our relationship with Jim Eisenbraun rewarding and enjoyable: his business acumen and attention to detail (known by all in the field), his genuine humanity (felt by all who know him), and his laid-back and unpretentious sense of humor, often expressed at his own expense.

To illustrate his subtle, at times dry and self-effacing humor, we quote directly, unadorned with commentary and in chronological order, from emails received from Jim over the past three years. It was during this time that we were coming to an agreement with Eisenbrauns for publishing our seasonal reports and then processing those publications.

3 June 2016
Dear Doug and Larry (#1) and Larry (#2):
I'll let you-all sort out who is #1 and who is #2; not my problem!
Doug has nudged me, now that he's (briefly) in the U.S.; and I confess that this topic was moved to the back burner for a few weeks as I dealt with stuff boiling over on other burners; but it remained on the stove, if cooling off significantly. Anyway …

23 August, 2016
Sorry to be slow to reply; I had a very busy weekend, and then Monday was Monday.

24 August 2016
Dear Doug, Larry 1, and Larry 2:
(I'll let the Larries, or is it Larrys? sort out who's #1.)
Well, obviously, I didn't get to this yesterday afternoon, as promised. I apologize; my brain turned to mush mid-afternoon …

14 December 2016
Dear Monique:
Very good! We'll let you know if anything at all changes on our end of things, though these dates seem perfectly fine to me. We'll plan on hosting you on Thursday January 19, barring inclement weather or other things not under our control!
Warmly, on a cold morning here in Indiana (slightly below zero F, or about -19 C this a.m.)

2 May 2017
We can certainly discuss this; color is both useful and quite helpful in making certain things clear. But sometimes creative ways of dealing with the inability to produce color can achieve the same effect without being as "pretty."
(Bear in mind that an archaeological final report will sell perhaps 100 units in the first year, and publishers need to make their investment in the publication back within that period of time, or else it would be better just to invest in the stock market.)

18 July 2017
A blurb: what we need, for our website particularly, but also for any other potential advertising, is a well-written, gushing description of the book and its contents: what does it cover? why is this the best-book-yet in the series? and so on. If you want to knock this around among the 4 of you and then send something to us, that's fine. We need about 250–300 words; more than that, and people will stop reading. And be effusive!

18 July 2017
So, it's "Larry #1"! or are you "Larry #2"?

3 October 2017
Unless the world ends (something one thinks about these days), the book will certainly be at ASOR.

9 April 2019
I think it should be sans comma (more naturally reading "Stratum 10 pottery" (no pause in breathing/speaking/reading).

9 April 2019
Monique:
Thanks for the explanations and the ID file (sent separately). So that I don't screw anything up, can you send me a new PDF for the front matter? That way, I can be certain that I don't have any font or other issues messing with your good work!

15 July 2019
Yep. The Eisenbrauns imprint will continue to live, and so all books published by Eisenbrauns as a PSU Press imprint get referred to as: Blah blah blah blah. University Park, PA: Eisenbrauns, 0000.

JODI MAGNESS
University of North Carolina at Chapel Hill

I HAVE PUBLISHED THREE VOLUMES WITH JIM: A FINAL EXCAVATION report; a monograph; and a co-edited festschrift. My department at UNC expects candidates for tenure and promotion to publish a monograph in a "good university press." However, university presses generally have no interest in technical archaeological volumes, preferring instead more "synthetic" studies without the numerous plans and section drawings, photographs, and line drawings of pottery and other finds that are part of a field work report. Perhaps Jim's greatest contribution to Near Eastern archaeology was publishing the results of archaeological projects that most other presses are unwilling to consider.

The publication of field work data is the most important thing that we as archaeologists do, for this is how we share with others information about remains that were destroyed during the excavation process. Jim performed an invaluable service to Near Eastern archaeology by providing a high-quality publication outlet for specialty studies, and selling the volumes at a reasonable price.

DANIEL M. MASTER
Wheaton College

IT WAS THE FIRST EMAIL THAT I RECEIVED FROM JIM. MY TEAM HAD done years of archaeological work—finding old plans, overseeing the drawing of innumerable sherds, scanning photos, writing the synthetic prose. I thought we were pretty sophisticated and pretty close to being finished with our site report. Then we submitted the files to Eisenbrauns, and Jim gave it to me straight— your use of Adobe illustrator in these files was "a bit like using a turning lathe to, well, design a whole car, not just the axles and the drive-shaft." The metaphor was down to earth but at the same time clearly articulated that whatever I knew about archaeology, the world of publishing was wholly different. I might have a manuscript and fancy computer program, but without a knowledge of the details of publishing, I was just making a mess of it. Nothing was ever going to turn out right.

What happened next, however, was Jim's true gift. He and his team knew publishing *and* archaeology, he was one of the only people who got what the final result was supposed to look like from the perspective of *both* fields. He was used to dealing with archaeologists out their depth, and as he dealt with our manuscript, he was able to transform it into something that showed our work in the best possible light. This was Jim's gift to our field for more than forty years. He could recognize good work, even if it was not in the best shape when it received it; he could deal with the idiosyncrasies of the ancient Near Eastern community of scholars, and he could repeatedly produce volumes that showed the field at its best.

Working with Jim has been an education in the best sense. I've learned an immense amount about the field and about producing archaeological site reports, but, at the same time, it has always been clear that the wisest move is to trust him and to rely on his advice. We are currently collaborating on our ninth archaeological volume together, and every one of them shows his contribution. Who else could help us with color correction, odd catalog layouts, paper weight, various binding strategies for oddly sized illustrations, off-shore printing, and more.

I knew about none of these things and yet whenever we had a problem, Jim handled it with ease.

In a fundamental way, Jim has been at the nexus of ancient Near Eastern studies and archaeology as surely as any scholar in the field. The Eisenbrauns' contribution, stamped across the spine of so many volumes, has been central to our field's contribution to human knowledge for more than four decades. And at heart of all of this has been Jim's unique expertise and fundamental passion. It has been an honor to work with him.

MATTHEW MCAFFEE
Welch College

I HAVE ONLY BECOME AN ACQUAINTANCE OF JIM'S OVER THE PAST FEW years, but in that short time I have come to appreciate him in two significant ways. First, his commitment to providing a reputable and affordable publishing outlet for Near Eastern, archaeology, and biblical studies has been a major force in these fields. I became aware of this as a graduate student in Near Eastern studies and it has become increasingly apparent to me in my postgraduate work. Eisenbrauns is a standard-bearer for publishing in the field. Second, I am personally grateful to Jim for his willingness to take on younger scholars like myself. Many of the most recognizable names in the field of ancient Near Eastern studies have published volumes with Eisenbrauns, which speaks to its quality reputation. Yet Jim has been willing to provide opportunities for younger scholars as well. When I think of Jim Eisenbran, his attentive emails, gentle spirit, and warm smiles all loom large in my mind. I am grateful for his special role as a master editor and publisher, as well as a kind and gracious mentor and friend to so many of us.

CRAIG MELCHERT
University of California, Los Angeles

I FIRST MET JIM EISENBRAUN AT A MEETING OF THE AMERICAN ORIENTAL
Society (at least by 1997, if not earlier), where I learned of his leading
role in publishing the Society's *Journal* as well a wide variety of scholarly
works on virtually aspects of the ancient Near East. I came to know him
well and to fully appreciate his qualities as a person and editor/publisher
when he offered to publish Harry A. Hoffner Jr.'s and my co-authored
A Grammar of the Hittite Language as Volume 1 of his series Languages
of the Ancient Near East. The process of bringing the work to publication was long and complex, and Jim showed infinite patience with two
"alpha male" personalities who among other things felt no obligation
whatsoever to follow the dictates of *The Chicago Manual of Style*. When
it became clear that a much-needed index to the grammar itself in print
form would be a heavy burden for Harry and delay the appearance of the
book still further, Jim helpfully suggested and implemented a searchable
CD-ROM version of the text that accompanied every copy (with guide-
lines for use) that has proven most effective. He also saw to it that typos
discovered by the first users and reviewers of both the grammar and the
tutorial were corrected in the next printing. Jim also readily agreed to
the posting on the Eisenbrauns website and on our personal pages of
addenda & corrigenda to the grammar. The long delay in the appearance of the first installment was due to circumstances beyond his (and
my) control. I will always be most grateful for all of Jim's assistance and
enabling in bringing the *GrHL* to fruition with the quality of production
and affordable price for which Eisenbrauns is famous.

  I always enjoy meeting and chatting with Jim at the AOS meetings
every March and look forward to many more such happy encounters.

TRYGGVE METTINGER
Lund University

JIM, YOU ARE NOW ENTERING A NEW PHASE OF YOUR LIFE WHEN YOUR many decades long work with Eisenbrauns Publishing is completed history. Your lifelong publishing enterprise is history also above and beyond your personal history. When the history of the twentieth and twenty-first centuries of studies in the fields of biblical and ancient near eastern studies (incl. Egyptology) will be written, the role of Eisenbrauns publishing will stand out as more important than the accumulated efforts of busloads of scholars in these fields.

Receive my congratulations, Jim. Your professional life has meant so much to so many. For decades topnotch scholarship has emanated from Eisenbrauns and reached the four corners of the world in excellent graphic shape. You and Eisenbrauns have served the scholarly enterprise in a way that must be profoundly satisfying to you and your whole crew of highly qualified staff personnel.

Besides, your marketing of various contributions published in other parts of the world has meant much in terms of convenient access for all of us.

Let me say from my personal perspective: It has been a pleasure and a comfort to experience the cooperation of Eisenbrauns publishing. With the recent publication of my collected essays you gave my own professional life cycle a rounding off that filled me with happiness.

I wish you, Jim, and your family many fine years, lived at a pace that is a bit less hectic that your life use to be, years that involve the blessing of aging with grace and finding new aspects of our human existence to enjoy.

ERIC M. MEYERS AND CAROL MEYERS
Duke University

ERIC: I AM HAPPY TO SAY THAT IN THE EARLY 1980S I WAS A WITNESS to a major step in the growth of Eisenbraun's publishing enterprise. As newly appointed First Vice-President for Publications of the American Schools of Oriental Research (ASOR), my first real assignment was to go to Ann Arbor, close up the ASOR Publications office that was located there at the time, and see what equipment and supplies could be salvaged. David Noel Freedman, my predecessor as head of ASOR publications, was stepping down from that position after many years; but he was not particularly happy about losing it as a platform for his various activities. Noel, to whom I had grown close because of Carol's and my involvement in the Anchor Bible, in fact wanted no part of closing down ASOR's Ann Arbor office. So basically it was Jim Eisenbraun and I who closed the office and divided up its contents. Jim had been Noel's right hand man for years and no doubt learned much about academic publication from him. But someone else taught him to be a perfect gentleman, for it was a delight to work with him.

There were two huge and heavy typesetting machines in the Ann Arbor office at the time. We decided to send one to the University of Pennsylvania, where the *Journal of Cuneiform Studies* was then produced, and Jim kept the other to use in those formative years of Eisenbrauns. Not only did Jim and I become good friends through this early Ann Arbor experience, but we also established a close relationship between ASOR and Eisenbrauns—a relationship that continues to this day. Eisenbrauns became the near exclusive typesetter for ASOR in the next decades. From those modest beginnings. Eisenbrauns would soon become a household name in Near Eastern and biblical studies. I am proud to have been there in Eisenbrauns' formative years, and I am equally proud to have had his team publish two of our Meiron Excavation Project sites in Upper Galilee and all of our materials from Sepphoris in Lower Galilee.

CAROL: AS ERIC MENTIONS, EISENBRAUNS WAS THE PUBLISHER OF MANY of our final excavation reports. It may not be an understatement to say that publishing archaeological materials is among the most challenging tasks that a publisher faces. Dealing with all those photographs, charts, drawings, tables, and endless lists and data sets can indeed be daunting. Jim Eisenbraun was unfailingly honest, timely, and professional in all our interactions as we negotiated the many details involved in establishing the costs, schedule, format, and processes involved in producing an archaeological volume. Our published reports accomplished everything we hoped they would, in no small part because of Jim's expertise and advice. It was always a pleasure to work with him, and we are grateful to have had him as a partner in the culminating aspect—publication—of our archaeological projects.

WILLIAM E. MIERSE
University of Vermont

I ONLY MET JIM ONE TIME, BUT IT WAS AN IMPORTANT MEETING FOR me. I had just written a book-length manuscript on temples produced in the ancient Levant in the centuries of the Early Iron Age. It was not my first book, but it represented a major move, since I have been working almost exclusively on Roman material, particularly Roman religious architecture on the Iberian Peninsula. This new manuscript had been a stretch for me, and now I was trying to find a publisher willing to take a chance with it.

Jim was that person. He graciously agreed to meet with me during meetings in Boston. I was unsure of what to expect, but was happily surprised to engage with such a warm and jovial individual with a good sense of humor and open demeanor. He had read the description of the text and was interested to learn about me and wanted to know why I had chosen to move in this new direction. The idea of producing a book from a scholar who would be looking at the material from a different perspective excited him, and our meeting resulted in my sending him the complete manuscript. There was much work that I needed to do to make it suitable for the Eisenbraun name, but Jim was encouraging, and I went forward. The book that together we produced, *Temples and Sanctuaries from the Early Iron Age Levant, Recovery after Collapse*, became one of the titles in a new series, History, Archaeology, and Culture of the Levant, and remains one of my proudest scholarly achievements. I owe that to Jim Eisenbraun who was willing to take the risk on an author working outside of his normal sphere, and I wish more publishers would be as brave as Jim so as to encourage wider intellectual investigations.

ALAN MILLARD
University of Liverpool

JIM EISENBRAUN HAS COME TO THE END OF MAKING MANY BOOKS!
Some scholars' spouses may be grateful, but many, many scholars owe
a great debt of gratitude to the man who has enabled them to publish their work faster and better than they would expect. From selling
books to students at low prices to producing high quality, academic
tomes, Jim created a remarkable business. My shelves bear many valued
volumes with his imprint. All who dealt with him will have appreciated
his integrity and fairness, coupled with an innate courtesy. May he now
have time to read!

ROBERT D. MILLER II
The Catholic University of America

THE ONLY THING THAT PREVENTS ME FROM SAYING JIM WAS THE FINEST editor I've ever worked with was having worked with David Noel Freedman as an editor. Since Jim was unlikely to provide his editorial feedback on a typewriter, the comparison would be apples to oranges.

Jim was above all else a thorough editor. His meticulous attention to every detail from maps to French capitalization rules ensured that every Eisenbrauns book in a very real sense had his name on it. Although this painstaking editing could be pain-full for an author, in the end the final product was worth the toil. What is more, that scrupulous approach to editing guaranteed that Jim was an advocate for the author when necessary in altercations with copy editors who might not really grasp what the work was attempting.

My greatest gratitude to Jim is for his willingness to take risks. When my *Dragon* book promised to leave hanging an appendix too large for inclusion but too large for most journal articles, Jim encouraged me to consider publishing it separately with Eisenbrauns, in spite of the fact that the subject matter was St. George—hardly standard ancient Near East fare. I suspect it was one of the last books Jim had a serious hand in the completion of, but I'm thrilled he convinced me and the series editors that it belonged with the imprint.

CYNTHIA L. MILLER-NAUDÉ
University of the Free State

I HAVE BEEN PRIVILEGED TO KNOW JIM EISENBRAUN AS A STUDENT, AN employee, and a colleague, though these labels do not begin to encompass the ways in which he positively impacted my life. I first met Jim Eisenbraun as one of his Hebrew students. He was not my first teacher of Hebrew, but both what he taught and the way that he taught have shaped the ways in which I attempt to teach Hebrew. Studying Hebrew with Jim involved not just Hebrew, but also linguistics, comparative Semitics, and ancient Near Eastern archaeology and culture—a new world beyond that of the biblical text opened up.

While a student, Jim hired me to work for his fledgling publishing company as a typesetter and later copy editor in the summer of 1980. There was only one typesetting machine and it was already running two shifts, from seven in the morning to eleven at night. I was therefore hired for the graveyard shift from eleven to seven. The volume *Hebrew Verse Structure* by Michael Patrick O'Connor—the first Eisenbraun volume to be published—was being typeset. We also worked on the typesetting of a massive archaeological volume for the University of Chicago Press. In those days, typesetting involved physically typing from a paper manuscript and nothing was automatic. To typeset the numerous tables in the archaeology volume, tedious and meticulous calculations of picas and points were required in order to manually determine the width of each column. Even footnotes were not automatically placed at the bottom of the page. For the special characters involved in transliterating Semitic languages, special programming of the typesetting machines were required to precisely place the diacritic over or under the letter in each typeface. Typesetting Hebrew required typing backwards and then making sure that the phrase or sentence did not break across a line, resulting in the Hebrew words in the wrong order. In spite of these difficulties, Jim produced beautifully typeset volumes at very affordable prices. Publishing was never about making money, but rather about serving the academic discipline by disseminating knowledge.

In the mid 1980s, production began on the Waltke and O'Connor, *Introduction to Biblical Hebrew Syntax*. Jim wanted to produce a volume that would not only be a classic grammar for its content, but also for its physical characteristics. He therefore asked a group of us to collect an assortment of classic Semitic grammars (e.g. Gardiner's Egyptian grammar, Von Soden's Akkadian grammar) and examine the typographical composition of each one. From this he then worked to determine the physical characteristics of the Waltke and O'Connor layout—the size of the pages, the size of type, the leading, the offset of Hebrew and English examples, etc.—and sample pages were made to refine the stylesheet. Jim himself did all or nearly all of the typesetting. The result was a truly classic grammar in every sense of the word.

As a colleague, it has been a privilege to work with Jim on various publishing projects. Since its inception, I have worked with him as one of the co-editors of Linguistic Studies in Ancient West Semitic, first with Michael Patrick O'Connor and then with Jacobus Naudé. I also edited two volumes that he published—*The Verbless Clause in Biblical Hebrew: Linguistic Approaches* and *Diachrony in Biblical Hebrew* (with Ziony Zevit). It is really a pleasure to have a publisher who intimately knows the academic field as well as the intricacies of all aspects of the publishing process and who is always ready to give good advice for solving any problem.

Finally, I have valued Jim and Merna's friendship over these many years. Although it is hard to imagine continuing academic and publishing endeavours without his input and support, I wish both of them a very enjoyable retirement.

BETH ALPERT NAKHAI
The University of Arizona

IT IS AN HONOR AND A PLEASURE TO WRITE IN CELEBRATION OF JIM
Eisenbraun. Jim has, for decades, been a pillar in our broad and complex
fields—supportive of publishing ventures, generous with his knowledge,
and kind. The books that Eisenbrauns has published over these many
years are counted among the firmament in our bibliophilic world; they
remain assets to us all. Jim's press will live on as an imprint of Penn State
University Press—but PSU Press will never replace Jim Eisenbraun.
    As for many of us, my interactions with Jim have been various. At
the annual ASOR meetings, he—and Merna, too—have been hospitable
guides to Eisenbrauns' myriad publications. I have co-edited two books
that Eisenbrauns published (*Household Religion: Toward a Synthesis of
Old Testament Studies, Archaeology, Epigraphy, and Cultural Studies;
Proceedings of the International Conference at Westfälisches Wilhelms-
Universität Münster, April 1st-3rd, 2009* [2014]; and, *Celebrate Her for
the Fruit of Her Hands: Studies in Honor of Carol L. Meyers* [2015]). The
guidance that Jim provided was invaluable to the success of both. The
same can be said about a prepublication review session that I chaired
at an annual meeting of the Society of Biblical Literature, which discussed Rainer Albertz and Rüdiger Schmitt's then-forthcoming *Family
and Household Religion in Ancient Israel and the Levant* (2012). Six of
the articles that I have published in the past fifteen years have been
in Eisenbrauns books. Until I began thinking about this tribute, I had
never quantified these publications, but they stand as a testimony to the
impact Jim has had on me—and on the work we all do.
    I want to comment, as well, on a different kind of contribution that
Jim has made. Eisenbrauns has been a—perhaps, the—major publisher
of honorary volumes, those collections of articles that commemorate
luminaries in our various fields of study. They are special volumes,
which offer colleagues and former students the opportunity to share
their scholarship, and to reflect on the impact that the honoree has had
on that scholarship, and on their professional—and sometimes personal—development. Assisting the editors in wresting these articles

from their authors and crafting them into volumes worthy of publication, volumes that credit the honorees, is no simple task. Jim's hand in this strong portfolio has been exceptional and bears mention. Jim's contribution to all our scholarly endeavors is vast. I wish him a future of joy, well-earned relaxation, and, of course, continuing erudition.

JACOBUS A. NAUDÉ
University of the Free State, South Africa

JIM EISENBRAUN, THE MAKER OF GOOD BOOKS

WORKING IN THE SOUTH AFRICAN CONTEXT WHERE BIBLIOPHOBIA, that is the strong dislike of books, especially by university authorities and librarians—to state it softly—is the order of the day, I myself as a booklover have huge respect for a fellow booklover, Jim Eisenbraun. My esteem is even greater for him, because he produced quality books for decades, which enrich in a considerable way my academic life and that of my students. Of all the books published by Eisenbrauns, I have never found a single weak one. On the contrary, they are treasure troves loaded with information and each volume is still relevant for the 21st century. One example of the many useful Festschriften on my shelves is, for example, *The Word of the Lord Shall Go Forth*, which was published in 1983. Researching and teaching Biblical Hebrew linguistics in its Ancient Near Eastern and Mediterranean context, it is not surprising that the books published by Eisenbrauns are the majority of books on my personal shelves as well as that of the library of the little shot institution where I am employed. In fact, although books at my university library are on the endangered species list, I can report that none of the books by Eisenbrauns are weeded at this stage. John Milton (1608–1674) is very informative in this regard: "As good almost kill a man as kill a good book: who kills a man kills a reasonable creature, God's image; but he who destroys a good book, kills reason itself, kills the image of God, as it were in the eye".

There is enormous evidence that Jim's achievement as a publisher embodies the Eisenbrauns slogan: "More than 35 years of good books." It pus him in good company with people like John Milton, who stated that "a good book is the precious life-blood of a master spirit, embalmed and treasured up on purpose to a life beyond life"; Thomas Carlyle (1795–1881), who said that "a good book is the purest essence of a human mind"; and, Martin Farquhar Tupper (1810–1889), with the slogan "A good book is the best of friends, the same to-day and for ever."

According to Merriam-Webster the first known use of the word *booklover* was in 1756. If Jim had lived before this date, there would surely be an earlier dating for this word. In his *Dictionary of Word Origins*, John Ayto claims that the original meaning of the word *book* in Old English was simply a "written document or record," and that it was only by the 9th century that it had been applied to a collection of written sheets fastened together. If Jim had lived in the 9th century the definition of *book* would undoubtedly be far more sophisticated. Before this date the dominant forms of written media were the tablet (clay, wax), stone, ostraca, scroll and codex (papyrus, parchment, and paper). Since such texts were often not written by the hand of the author, but were dictated by the author to a secretary or scribe, what role would Jim have had, if he had lived during those times?

In 1440 the world changed dramatically to print communication and typographic interpretive culture with the invention of printing by Johann Gutenberg, arguably the most important event of the past 1000 years. Since the 1960s the role of the computer and the mobile device— the screen—brought a new revolution which led to electronic media communication or digital-media interpretive culture. Jim is fortunate to live in an era in which he could utilize the full cycle of "book" history to publish the actual handwritten and manuscript documents in book and digital formats as well as the modern studies which accompany them.

I have known and utilized the books of Eisenbrauns since the 1980s, but was fortunate to meet him in person for the first time in 2009 when I was invited to a meal with him where he asked me to be co-editor with Cynthia Miller of the book series Linguistic Studies in Ancient West Semitic, of which volume 15 is just published. Many meals followed at the SBL meetings as well as in Winona Lake. I was always impressed by the wisdom of the decisions Jim made concerning publications. One can only hope that PennState Press will carry forward the legacy of Jim Eisenbraun for the benefit of our academic field.

Jim Eisenbraun can be proud of what he has achieved. Enjoy your retirement!

BENJAMIN J. NOONAN
Columbia International University

JIM EISENBRAUN'S IMPACT ON THE ACADEMY CANNOT BE OVERSTATED. He exemplifies professionally the same excellence that characterizes each and every Eisenbrauns book. Jim is committed to publishing works that are of the highest quality and that make significant scholarly contributions to our field. His relentless pursuit of excellence was evident throughout the publication process for both books I have published with Eisenbrauns, and I know that my experience is not unique. It is not too much to say that my field of study—Hebrew Bible and ancient Near Eastern Studies—would not be where it is today were it not for the books he has published.

Jim also exemplifies excellence at a personal level. He has a high concern not only for the books he produces, but also for the people who have authored those books. In all my interactions with Jim, he has always been friendly, eager to help, and encouraging. I will not forget the time that he personally contacted me just after one of my books had been published. Although he did not have to do so, he took the time to offer his hearty congratulations and encourage me on my book's publication. Jim's small acts of kindness, which ultimately flow from his care for his authors, set him apart from other publishers and make him a model of excellent character to which we should all aspire.

PAM NICHOLS
Typesetter and Proofreader, 1981–1989; Prepress Manager, 1989–2019

I CAME TO WORK AT EISENBRAUNS IN OCTOBER OF 1981 WITH A background of teaching special education. I knew Jim as my husband's Hebrew professor in seminary and Merna as part of the seminary women's group. At that time, Eisenbrauns was doing prepress work for a handful of journals and just beginning to publish reprints of out of print titles. Jim managed everything himself and hired typesetters and a few salespeople, mainly seminary students and their spouses. The business grew and evolved before our eyes until Eisenbrauns was a premier publisher known around the world. Jim Eisenbraun worked harder than any of the employees and burned a lot of midnight oil. He deserves the credit for building a well-renowned business and for making the Eisenbraun imprint a gold standard for "quality books at a reasonable price." I had a safe and congenial place to work for nearly forty years in an interesting and challenging industry, thanks to Jim Eisenbraun. I'm glad I could play a part in the story. Cheers to you, Jim!

BEN C. OLLENBURGER
Anabaptist Mennonite Biblical Seminary

JIM EISENBRAUN HAS MADE A REMARKABLE, IMMENSELY VALUABLE contribution to scholarship in biblical studies and other fields, all of them related to his interest and expertise. Beginning as an importer and bookseller, he provided easy access to publications from Europe, especially Germany, at a time when—as Bruce Metzger once remarked—German was the most important Semitic language. Decades ago, while writing a dissertation, I thrilled to open a package from Eisenbrauns with Hans Wildberger's three German volumes on Isaiah. Among fledgling scholars at the time, Eisenbrauns was the indispensable source.

Before Amazon.com drove independent booksellers into oblivion, I took a group of interested students to visit the Eisenbrauns publishing facility and its immense warehouse, near the shores of Winona Lake in Indiana. The students were amazed to find volumes on Sumerian orthography next to Emar excavation reports and not far from books on contemporary Judaism and Christianity. Jim Eisenbraun encompasses worlds.

An author or editor of any Eisenbrauns publication knows what a privilege it has been to work with Jim. For good reason, scholars from around the world count Jim as a friend. At the same time, Jim demands excellence. He is a lover of language, and of several languages, and as a publisher he has an editor's eye. The editors who worked with Jim at Eisenbrauns followed his expert eye in producing work of the highest quality.

That quality extended to the actual printing of books in Eisenbrauns' own plant. No press, here or abroad, produced books of higher *material* quality, let alone doing so of sometimes-arcane volumes with a severely limited market and selling them at a price that would still make them accessible. Jim published books as a scholarly and humane mission in service to the academy, broadly and generously defined. He has served the academy—served us—well, and he has done so as a friend. A good friend.

DAVID I. OWEN
Cornell University

I NO LONGER REMEMBER WHEN I FIRST MET JIM EISENBRAUN BUT IT was clearly when he was still in graduate school and when he was creating Xerox copies of old publications to facilitate the study of his fellow graduate students and friends. This, no doubt, planted the seeds that grew into the major ancient Near Eastern/biblical studies publisher in the United States. Since that time, Jim (usually along with his wife, Merna) and I met regularly at the AOS, ASOR and SBL meetings and where we developed an enduring friendship through our mutual interests both in publishing and particularly in the field of Assyriology. Aside from trying (successfully I might add) to make a living as a publisher, Jim went out of his way to facilitate the publication of countless books, at reasonable prices, that might never have seen publication otherwise. As a result, the Eisenbraun's imprint was ever-present in the libraries of virtually everyone in the field of Near Eastern and biblical studies.

Jim's personal interest and involvement in every publication, his gracious demeanor, and his dedication to scholarly excellence found in the Eisenbraun's publications have been the hallmarks of his long and productive career as a publisher. Even now, as he retires, he continues to facilitate the transition to a new publisher, smoothing out the difficulties for both old and new authors. Our field owes Jim a great debt for the numerous, essential and enduring contributions to ancient Near Eastern and biblical studies in the United States. I wish him a well-earned healthy retirement and look forward to his continuing presence at our professional meetings for years to come.

SIMO PARPOLA
University of Helsinki

JIM EISENBRAUN HAS A SPECIAL PLACE IN MY MIND, ALTHOUGH OUR friendship has by necessity always been a business relationship only. Nevertheless, I consider Jim a true and trusted friend, who played a significant and beneficial part in my life for more than thirty years.

I came to know Jim in the early eighties from his book catalogues (primarily *Scholar's Source*), which soon became my main avenue to new books in the fields of Assyriology, ancient Near Eastern, and biblical studies. In 1986, I was lucky to initiate a major long-term project to publish the extant archival texts of the Neo-Assyrian Empire in a series of critical text editions, State Archives of Assyria (SAA), published by the Helsinki University Press. The first volume in the series appeared in 1987, but it soon became evident that the Press had difficulties in marketing the book properly. Impressed by Jim's efficiency as distributor, I decided in January 1989 to write to him and ask whether he would be willing to distribute the SAA series in U.S.A. and Canada. The answer was yes, and by the end of 1992, with eight SAA volumes published and distributed properly, our problems were over.

Encouraged by this, I ventured in 1993 to launch a new series, State Archives of Assyria Studies (SAAS), the first volume of which was printed at my own expense. This series was planned to become an open-ended channel for SAA related studies, the aim being to finance the printing of future volumes from sales returns, so that no further funding would be needed. To make this happen, it was of course essential that the series would be attractively and efficiently marketed and distributed, and I was extremely glad when Jim agreed to become its worldwide distributor in April 1993.

The new series grew up rapidly; by 1996, five SAAS volumes had been published, and in 1997 I was ready to start another new series, SAA Cuneiform Texts, financed in the same way and also exclusively distributed by Eisenbrauns. In the course of the following five years, several new volumes in the SAA, SAAS and SAACT series were published along with five volumes of *The Prosopography of the Assyrian*

Empire; one volume of SAA Literary Texts; the Proceedings of the 47th Rencontre Assyriologique Internationale held in Helsinki; and other monographs like the *Helsinki Atlas of the Near East in the Neo-Assyrian Period,* all except SAA again exclusively distributed by Eisenbrauns. This publishing activity would not have been possible without Jim.

I'll give just one example to illustrate how vital Jim's support was for the SAA Project. In February 2004, I had to turn to Jim with the following plea:

> Dear Jim,
> I am sorry to bother you in a matter that actually belongs to the sphere of responsibility of your sales manager. At the end of the year, we received a huge bill for shipping and storage (€12,500) from Vammala (our printers). We have not been able to pay this bill completely yet, and despite some recent income, our publishing account still remains in the red for the second consecutive month already. This means that unless we receive some substantial orders in the near future that will help turn the current negative balance into positive, I will no longer be able to keep Bob [Whiting] as our managing editor. Since the discontinuation of the Centre of Excellence funding at the end of 2001, our sole source of income has been the returns from the sales of our publications, and Bob's salary has been paid from our publishing account since September 2002.
> I am quite confident that our publishing activities will continue to be profitable in the future, but right now we need your help to keep us in business.
> We have two volumes of SAA Studies coming out in April and an *English-Assyrian-English Dictionary* later on. All these books, especially the dictionary, should sell well. In addition, an important SAACT volume is approaching completion. If you could place an advance order on these books soon plus replenish your stock on our earlier publications, we would be in the clear. I hope you can give us a hand in this critical situation.

Jim responded on the same day, faxed the orders I had requested, and in addition suggested a "money-making" idea for the future: licencing Eisenbrauns to produce out-of-print SAA volumes on a print-on-demand (POD) basis, with a royalty on each sale paid to the SAA

Project. It took four years to sell the idea to the University Press, but on May 2008, the project could finally begin.

In May 2009, we agreed to move the Project's inventory of books from Vammala to Eisenbrauns' storehouse in Winona Lake, to obviate the cost of shipping backlisted titles from Finland to U.S.A.

Starting with 2009, all our books were printed in U.S.A. in collaboration with Jim, and after Bob Whiting's retirement as managing editor in May 2011, I had to take his duties upon myself. It now became my task to monitor the preparation of manuscripts and covers, send final PDFs to Jim, write blurbs, and draw up mailing lists for review and complimentary copies; Jim's staff checked the manuscripts for layout and printability, supervised the printing and took care of shipping, billing and the rest. All this required frequent contact by email. I exchanged over 160 emails with Jim and many more with his staff.

Together, we published 17 books in 2011–2017: PNA 3/II (2011), SAAS 21 and SAA 19 (2012), SAACT 8–9 and SAAS 22 (2013), SAACT 10 (2014), SAAS 23 and SAACT 11 (2015), SAAS 24–25, *EDSL* 1–2, and SAACT 12 (2016), SAAS 26, PNA 4/I and SAA 20 (2017). Jim acquainted himself with every manuscript and helped me by his experience to decide about print runs and retail prices. I remember with particular gratitude the care that he took with my *Etymological Dictionary of the Sumerian Language,* which was submitted for publication in January 2016.

It was a shock to me to learn from Jim in October 2017 that Eisenbrauns had been acquired by the Penn State University Press and was henceforward to continue as its Imprint. This decision signalled the end of an almost 30 years old business relationship and involved all sorts of serious problems for the continuation of our publishing activities. Luckily, all these problems have now been sorted out, and I am glad to have been able to establish, with Jim's help, a good relationship with PSU Press. Under its aegis, four further SAA and SAAS volumes have been published in the past two years.

Thank you, Jim. I really enjoyed working with you.

JÖRG PERSCH
Brill Deutschland

JIM, I DO NOT EXACTLY REMEMBER WHEN WE FIRST MET; IT WILL
probably have been towards the end of 2005. At that time I was working
with Vandenhoeck & Ruprecht, and we were looking for a distribution
in the USA. This was followed by a three-year collaboration, in which
Eisenbrauns distributed V&R in the USA until we decided to set up
our own subsidiary in the USA.

Already at our first meetings I was impressed by your enthusiasm.
Unlike most publishers, Eisenbrauns has copy-edited books and journals page by page. This was highly valued by the authors and put us
competing publishers under a certain pressure to justify ourselves. On
all my visits to Winona Lake I felt the pride of your team in the quality of your products. And you can say with the same pride that you
have promoted science over four decades and improved it through
sustainable, carefully selected publications. And even if you don't find
Eisenbrauns books on every academic desk, at least your mugs are
indispensable there.

In 2007, from 15 to 20 July then, we met at the IOSOT in Ljubljana.
I think we can say that we became friends there over dinner and long
conversations. Although we have rarely seen each other more than
three times a year since then, it always feels as if it was yesterday. We
have also shared our respective professional crises, at least with mutual
advice and attention.

Now you have found a good new home for your publishing house,
even though I would have found it wonderful if we had once again
found a way to work together. But:

Ὦ βάθος πλούτου
καὶ σοφίας καὶ γνώσεως θεοῦ·
ὡς ἀνεξεραύνητα τὰ κρίματα αὐτοῦ
καὶ ἀνεξιχνίαστοι αἱ ὁδοὶ αὐτοῦ.

It's really hard to believe that you will retire. But I hope that you can give your creativity more room and that this will not get on Merna's nerves too much. A motorcycle license would be a good plan. The leather jacket will suit you especially well. By the way, I wear the T-shirt that you see here under mine.

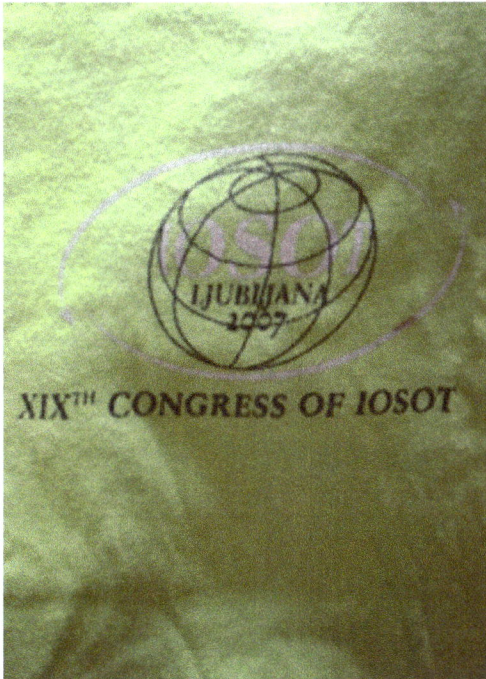

BEZALEL PORTEN
Hebrew University of Jerusalem

BEGINNINGS ARE OFTEN SHROUDED IN MYSTERY, SO I DON'T KNOW
when exactly Jim and I first got together. All I remember is that Eisenbrauns marketed our *TAD* volumes. After I published my expanded
doctoral dissertation, "Archives from Elephantine," I was inspired by
Tcherikover's *Corpus Papyrorum Iudaicarum* to produce a *Corpus
Papyrorum Aramaicarum*. It was intended to replace Cowley and
Kraeling and Aimé-Giron. I thought it was a project that could be done
in a year or so and applied for and received an NEH grant to achieve
it. But then I met Ada Yardeni, graphic artist and paleographer, and
the project took on a whole new dimension. Beginning with the Bisi-
tun Inscription, we went on to publish four volumes, which we named
*Textbook of Aramaic Documents from Ancient Egypt, Newly Copied,
Edited and Translated into Hebrew and English* (1986–1999). It became
known as *TAD* and indeed replaced Cowley and Kraeling. We went to
libraries and museums from Moscow to Brooklyn, tracing and hand-
copying every Aramaic piece we could find. We divided the finds by
content: letters, contracts, literary texts, ostraca, and other inscriptions.
The method of publication was cut and paste and the publisher was
the inhouse Academon. The worldwide distributor was Eisenbrauns. I
bought the copies from the Academon and sold them to Eisenbrauns
and they duly and truly marketed them. Somewhere, each of us has a
record of when this procedure began and when it came to an end, but
neither can recall it exactly. Anyway, by making the volumes available
all over, Eisenbrauns played a major role in elevating TAD to the status
of the standard publication of Aramaic texts of Persian period Egypt.
It has since spawned a KWIC, edited by me and Jerome Lund, and a
grammar, edited by Takamitsu Muraoka and myself; and inspired the
Brill/SBL publication *The Elephantine Papyri in English*, which I edited.

I was on the way to doing a revised edition of my 1968 "Archives"
when the unprovenanced Aramaic Idumean ostraca came on the stage.
Uncovered at unknown sites (or site), they were acquired by collec-
tors, who put them at the disposal of scholars for publication. In 1996,

there appeared two such, one by Israel Eph'al and Joseph Naveh and another by André Lemaire, who produced a second volume in 2002. Meanwhile, for almost ten years, from 2003 to 2012, Yardeni and I had published ten articles on these ostraca. The time was ripe to classify and publish the whole corpus of some 2,000 pieces, to be called, on the model of *TAD*, *Textbook of Aramaic Ostraca from Idumea* (*TAO*). But unlike *TAD*, which had only handcopies and no photographs, *TAO* would be presented with photo, handcopy, Aramaic transcription and English translation, ceramic description and commentary. Publishing had entered the digital age, and there were separate files for the photos, for the hand drawings, for the Aramaic, and for the English texts. Moreover, someone had to do the formatting, bringing together the separate files and insuring that each ostracon would be on a separate page. Not without hesitation, I approached Eisenbrauns, and much to my delight, Jim responded affirmatively. His only question was, What do I say to those who claim these unprovenanced ostraca are forgeries? Many years later, I learned from a leading scholar that his approval had been sought. Fortunately, the ostraca were so unique that there was barely a model from which a forger could work.

When the work began, the question was, Should the photos be in black and white or in color? The latter would, of course, make the book more expensive, so I was surprised when the first proofs arrived with the photos in color. "The ostraca deserved to be in color," said Jim, and the cost difference was negligible. It wasn't easy reading proofs, because you always discovered something the umpteenth time around that you hadn't seen before, but Jim was patient and we went through six sets. He did a marvelous job of formatting. At the top were photo and handcopy, side by side. Beneath them were Aramaic text and English translation, also side by side. The English translation did not follow line for line the Aramaic word order, but a word order that made sense in English, with superscript numeration to indicate the Aramaic word order. In addition, there were marginal captions in a different font to indicate the subject. At the bottom the width of the page stood the ceramic description and the commentary. If the latter ran onto a second page, the bottom of that page was left blank, so that the next ostracon began at the top of the next full page. Hebrew and Aramaic words were always in Hebrew script and not in transliteration. If something didn't make sense, Jim was quick to point it out, and he didn't hesitate to raise questions.

The largest number of ostraca were commodity chits and we had arranged the thousand-some such according to family dossiers. As we were collecting and processing the material, I had concluded that having reached fifty, we should go to press. But having reached some 520 pages with just over 400 chits and a very long introduction, Jim decided that amount would suffice. Volume 2 with dossiers 11–50 thus contained some 370 pages and 263 chits. The *TAD* volumes came at three-, four-, and six-year intervals (1983, 1986, 1993, 1999), but the *TAO* volumes are coming at two-year intervals (2014, 2016, 2018, and 2020 to be published). Volume 3 was done under the imprimatur of Penn State Press, put together by Amy Becker. But the format was identical, for she had been trained by Jim.

Unlike the *TAD* volumes, *TAO* has no index, but volume 1 has an enclosed CD with three KWICS, one for words, one for PNs, and one for months. The idea for this disk came from Jim.

MURRAY RAE
University of Otago

IT HAS BEEN A GREAT PRIVILEGE TO WORK WITH YOU, JIM. WE HAVE
worked together on the *Journal of Theological Interpretation* and the JTI
Supplement Series. Thanks to Joel Green's initiative and your enthusiastic reception of the idea, the Journal is now in its 13th year and is
continuing to flourish. We have also published seventeen monographs
in the Supplement Series. Both projects have relied heavily upon and
benefited enormously from your personal attention. Your interest in
and dedication to the details of our small project, and the personal
advice and assistance given to authors while simultaneously taking care
of the publishing company as a whole has been quite extraordinary. It
has made my job as editor of the series, and briefly of the Journal, a
great deal more straightforward, and pleasurable, than it might otherwise have been. The production quality that you and your team have
delivered has been superb. I hope that I along with the other editors
and contributors to the Journal and Supplement Series have been able
to deliver material of sufficient quality to honour your commitment to
JTI. Your generous support of our labours has always been delivered
with admirable patience, kindness and good humour.

   I will also remember with gratiutude your generous hospitality at
the Annual Meetings of SBL and AAR. All of this leads to my offering
of heartfelt thanks Jim. It has been a great pleasure to work with you
through these past thirteen years. I wish you well and God's blessing
upon whatever it is that you will turn your attention to in retirement.

GARY A. RENDSBURG
Rutgers University

THE YEAR IS 1975: GARY RENDSBURG STARTED GRADUATE SCHOOL AT New York University, and Jim and Merna Eisenbraun started their business. Since I was in New York City, I was blessed with a number of excellent libraries: New York University, Columbia University, Jewish Theological Seminary, Hebrew Union College, and New York Public Library, all within walking distance of my domicile or a single subway ride away. As such, every book that I needed to consult during my graduate studies (ranging from Egyptology to Hebrew Studies to Assyriology to Semitic Languages) was available to me.

But if I was going to make a career in the academy, I also realized that I needed to start to build my own personal library. But how did one do so? There was no internet, and even email did not yet exist. Buying books from the U.S. university presses and publishers specializing in biblical studies was not an issue. As soon as one became a member of SBL or AOS or ASOR, one received flyers and catalogues in the mail on a regular basis.

But how did one go about buying books published in Europe and in Israel? Let's start with something as basic as *Ugaritic Textbook* (1967), written by my own teacher, Cyrus Gordon, a *sine qua non* for my graduate studies, and at the time the only all-inclusive grammar, text edition, and lexicon of the Ugaritic language. How did one obtain a copy from the Pontifical Biblical Institute in Rome? How did one issue payment? Did one simply send a letter accompanied by a U.S. check to Rome and hope for the best? And what about Israel? For example, the very important volume, *The Book of Ben Sira*, published by the Academy of the Hebrew Language (1973). Ditto, did one simply send a letter with a U.S. check enclosed to Jerusalem?

Into this state of affairs—call it a void, even—now 44 years ago, stepped the newly established enterprise, Eisenbrauns. I no longer remember how or when I first learned about the company, nor how I got on the company's mailing list. Perhaps at a conference? Perhaps from a fellow graduate student? Perhaps from one of my teachers?

Regardless, once I did learn about Eisenbrauns, and once I was on the mailing list, I still recall—indeed very vividly 40-plus years later—the excitement (yes, excitement, not too strong a word) each time one of those white brochures arrived from Eisenbrauns. In the first few pages, were half-page announcements of newly published and newly available books, while in the remainder of the brochure were long lists of books, arranged by category (Bible, Ugaritic, archaeology, etc.), published in years past, but in stock and also available for purchase. Not only that, but the prices were reasonable and affordable, even for a lowly graduate student living on a modest stipend. And for those of us who love geography, we all needed to find Winona Lake, Indiana, on the map! (No, not Google Maps, a real map!)

Eventually, Eisenbrauns expanded from selling and distributing books to publishing books of their own. When it came time for me to publish my first book, *The Redaction of Genesis* (1986), I turned to Eisenbrauns. The entire process was a pleasure: working with Jim and his staff, editing the manuscript, reading the professionally produced proofs, and determining the cover art. Twenty-eight years later, it was an equally pleasant experience to work with Eisenbrauns on the reprint of the book, with a new foreword (2014).

Along the way, there were many other collaborations with Eisenbrauns, including: four volumes of the *Eblaitica* series, coedited by Cyrus Gordon and myself (1987, 1990, 1992, 2002), and more recently, another coedited volume (with James Hoffmeier and Alan Millard), *"Did I Not Bring Israel Out of Egypt?" Biblical, Archaeological, and Egyptological Perspectives on the Exodus Narratives* (2016).

And then there were the many Eisenbrauns volumes to which I contributed, *Linguistics and Biblical Hebrew* (ed. Walter Bodine), *Phonologies of Asia and Africa* (ed. Alan Kaye), *Morphologies of Asia and Africa* (ed. Alan Kaye), *Near Eastern Archaeology* (ed. Suzanne Richard), *Diachrony in Biblical Hebrew* (eds. Cynthia Miller-Naudé and Ziony Zevit), *Doubling and Duplicating in the Book of Genesis* (eds. Elizabeth Hayes and Karolien Vermeulen), as well as Festschriften for Georg Krotkoff, Shalom Paul, Jeffrey Tigay, and Victor Hurowitz.

Though there is more, because Eisenbrauns also has been responsible for the production of two journals to which I have contributed over the years: *Jewish Quarterly Review* and *Journal of the American Oriental Society*.

If you add this all up, I suspect that not a year has gone by when I was not in contact with Jim Eisenbraun personally and/or members of his professional staff. Planning edited volumes, reviewing manuscripts, reading proofs, producing indices—there was always some task at hand!

It is a pleasure to contribute to this volume in Jim's honor. He changed the world of biblical studies and ancient Near Eastern studies, and we are all the beneficiaries of his vision and good work.

Finally, right, so how did I obtain the two books mentioned above: *Ugaritic Textbook* and *The Book of Ben Sira*—among many others? My records do not go that far back, but I must imagine that they were shipped to me from nowhere else but Winona Lake, Indiana!

SUZANNE RICHARD
Gannon University

I WAS DELIGHTED TO RECEIVE AN INVITATION—AS A MEMBER OF THE prestigious "Eisenbrauns" author/editor family—to contribute to a volume celebrating Jim Eisenbraun, who enabled so many of us to publish our generally esoteric and limited-run scholarly volumes. What kind of press is that that does not require a 50,000 copy-run to accept one's proposal? The answer is Eisenbrauns! As a graduate student I was so grateful to the early Eisenbrauns, a start-up business that found copies of out-of-print books or hard-to-get excavation reports in particular. I continued (and continue) to rely on Eisenbrauns for those scholarly and/or esoteric books. From one of the highly specialized and grateful academics of the world, I would like to offer my voice in praise of Jim's contribution (and lifelong dedication) to the academic community. Over 50 years Eisenbrauns anchored the scholarly field of Near Eastern Studies and Jim, Merna , and Eisenbrauns deserve accolades heaped upon them.

Although I really only saw Jim at conferences, I feel like I have been friends with both him and Merna for years, surely a testament to their boundless collegiality and graciousness: they will both be sorely missed. Really, the Book Exhibit was the place to lobby interest in a book idea or proposal, and Jim was always open to discussing one's research and ideas, even if ultimately the answer was that Eisenbrauns was not a good fit (I won't mention that book).

My first book with Eisenbrauns is a case in point illuminating Jim's great talent for listening, considering, and helping/enabling a project to come to fruition. When approached about a wealth of articles I had in my possession—a situation due to the ultimate impossibility of publishing yet another encyclopedia on the ancient Near East—Jim was so gracious and helpful in discussing alternatives. Discussions led to the reconceptualization of the collection of 62 articles as an edited work, *Near Eastern Archaeology: A Reader*, 2003, a volume that became a text book, as well as a very readable resource for the scholar, student, and lay person alike. Kudos to Jim and his wonderful staff who helped bring the work to fruition. Not only am I grateful for Jim's intercession and salvaging of am important compendium of scholarship, but so happy that he (I think) submitted the volume to Choice for review, resulting in the American Library Association's Choice Award as an "Outstanding Academic Title for 2004." To Jim and his staff, thank you!

My second book experience with Jim stems from the publication of my third volume (publication date March 2020), *New Horizons in the Study of the Early Bronze III and Early Bronze IV of the Levant*. This edited collection of 23 articles from scholars working across the Levant, stems from two workshops held at ASOR in 2014 and 2015. As before, it was a casual talk with Jim at the ASOR meetings which eventuated in a proposal and a contract with Eisenbrauns. This work proved to be much more challenging for all sorts of reasons (one of which the transition to PSU), but I have to say Jim was very understanding and fair about certain problems, miscommunications, and delays along the way. Again, his long-time copy-editors, James and Debbie Spinti and other staff members, along with the PSU staff worked tirelessly to drive the volume to publication as soon as possible. I am delighted with the final result.

Finally, more accolades to Jim, this time for not deserting us (the esoteric scholars with small-copy runs) but assuring that one of our major avenues to disseminate scholarly books remains alive and well, thanks to the happy metamorphosis of Eisenbrauns Winona Lake, Indiana, to Eisenbrauns University Park, Pennsylvania. In the best of both worlds, this transition finds the humanities of the ancient world still safe and Jim and Merna enjoying a well-deserved retirement. My best to both of you in all your future endeavors.

CHRISTOPHER ROLLSTON
George Washington University

JIM EISENBRAUN AND HIS GIFTED TEAM AT EISENBRAUNS HAVE CERtainly impacted the field in a multitude of profound ways. Naturally, one thinks of the very high caliber of the many hundreds of fine volumes which have been published by Eisenbrauns through the decades. Indeed, it would be difficult to calculate the collective gravity and importance of these volumes to the field. Furthermore, Jim Eisenbraun always tried (and was able) to price his volumes fairly, resulting in wide accessibility across the field as well. For this too, we in the field owe him so much. Moreover, during my time as co-editor (with Eric Cline) of the *Bulletin of the American Schools of Oriental Research*, we have often marveled at the superlative preprint work (e.g., typesetting and layout) of Eisenbrauns. And *BASOR* is simply one of a number of journals which Jim and his team capably produced in this fashion.

But perhaps the part of Jim's work which I most admire, and which may even be the most enduring, is the legacy of his kind and gentle manner to scholars young and old, junior and senior, as he published the produce of our pens. Ultimately, it seems to me that Jim Eisenbraun has always considered Eisenbrauns to be a vocation, perhaps even a mission, not just a business. Scores of Eisenbrauns titles are part of my own personal library (as with so many of us), and each one reminds me of Jim the person, his kind words, his gentle voice, his vibrant smile, and his caring heart. He is a sage, a scholar, a man of kindness and generosity, and a dear and treasured friend. For him, I am so very grateful.

JACK M. SASSON
Vanderbilt University

UNDER A HALF CENTURY AGO, I KNEW THE NAME EISENBRAUN AS THE owner of a book distributing firm specializing in the Hebrew Bible and allied subjects, including Egyptology, Assyriology, and the like. It all changed in the late 70s and early 80s, when Jim and I began our first of several occasions to improve access to scholarship for professionals in the field. Here are fragments from the full story.

In the late 70s, I had come to be the ancient Near East (and Bible) editor for the *Journal of the American Oriental Society*. With the other sectional editors, we strove to improve the journal's format. For many subscribers, its format had made it unwieldy and difficult to range with other journals on a shelf. For Jim, the *Journal's* compositor, its unusual configuration forced a waste of paper, raising the price of composition. Given the AOS's proud attachment to bygone ways, we did not immediately succeed in altering it; but eventually it all worked out. In any library now, the *JAOS* sits nice and comfy among its peers. Through it all, Jim was there to prod gently, ready with the needed information, but always willing to suggest and to consider alternate approaches.

When, late in the 70s, Jim produced his first volume, a beautifully designed book on *Hebrew Verse Structure* (M. O'Connor), the first of over 600 volumes since then. I recognized then how unusual a partner was Jim among publishers when it came to fulfilling the commitment. Given his academic training in the profession (he briefly taught Hebrew and HB at a theological seminary), Jim knew what manuscripts would enrich the field and had connection with scholars who might be prodded into submitting a significant work. Additionally, Jim strove to present us books of agreeable esthetics no less than lasting value.

Since those early heroic days to tame the JAOS's format, Jim and I have had many a good lunch in which we traded tidbits on many aspects of scholarship as well as an occasional gossip. (To be honest, likely because of his upbringing, Jim was not very good at idle chatter.) How to improve access to decent works was certainly a core subject. Presently, the opportunity to do so came early in our present millennium, when I came to be president of the then newly-minted *International Association for Assyriology.*

The IAA had become the umbrella and host for the annual *Rencontre Assyriologique Internationale.* Yearly since the 1950s, Assyriologists and others in cognate fields (archaeology and historian of arts among them), would meet at a major center of research in Europe and North America to discuss their works. Whatever academic institution or unit sponsored the meetings would be charged with producing that year's proceedings. The burden to the organizing committee was enormous: Beyond collecting those papers (not always easy) and editing the studies, that committee also was charged with finding a publisher. As a result, the interval until publication, the format of the volumes, and the quality of their production ranged widely. In particular, the price of the printed volumes could be exorbitant, beyond the means of most scholars and certainly of students. Luckily, Jim was there to improve the situation.

The email exchanges and the phone consultations on this particular metamorphosis could fill dossiers. The IAA board consisted of many colleagues with different temperaments, requirements, and expectations. Each had a surfeit of opinions on each item under discussion. Throughout, Jim remained patient, calm, inventive, accommodating, and gracious. Some insisted on giving the sponsoring local committees the option to select another publication avenue, normally a deal breaker in this enterprise. It was not so for Jim. There and then, I learned from him how to keep the eye on the goal: In this case, to provide all who wish to purchase them an affordable set of proceedings, consistent in the editing process, and pleasing in format. The membership approved the final accord at the 2007 Russia RAI.

Since, there have been too many other moments of lovely interactions with Jim for me to recount on this occasion. But let me end on a note of gratitude for the manner in which Jim personally took on full responsibility for producing my book on the letters from Old Babylonian Mari (*From the Mari Archives*, 2015, 17). The manuscript was hirsute, with enough divisions and subdivisions to enrage a saint and more footnotes than were sensibly necessary. Many times, I imagined Jim giving up on its production. Throughout its relatively brief genesis and despite the many updates and corrections that I kept on posting him, however, Jim remained cool and welcoming, expressing the soothing opinion that each new salvo from me simply improved the final product. I remain proud of the book—not (just) for its contents, mind you, but for the esthetic pleasure it still gives me when holding it in my hands. In Paris for the latest *RAI* (2019), I learned of yet another reason to be grateful to our dear Jim, publisher extraordinaire for us all.

So Jim, I hope you will discover—as I did—that "retiring" is but an invitation to change into new tires. So, with Merna as always at your side, be ready to set off towards the best frontiers in human life.

ʿ*ad mē'â *k*ĕ'esrîm*, ḥabibi.

GLENN M. SCHWARTZ
Johns Hopkins University

JIM EISENBRAUN HAS BEEN AN ESSENTIAL AND STEADFAST PRESENCE IN the field of ancient Near Eastern Studies for many decades. Working with him in publishing two edited volumes in 1996 and 2012 was a remarkably smooth and hassle-free process. In fact, I don't remember any significant frustrations, delays, or hang-ups. In the 1996 volume, Jim worked very conscientiously to ensure that the chapters were consistent, coherent, and intelligible. For the 2012 volume, I fondly recall Jim and me going back and forth about the cover, finally settling on something suitably lurid. In this as elsewhere, Jim's attention to detail and his imagination were remarkable. I also looked forward to seeing Jim at scholarly conferences (AOS, ASOR, etc.)—it was great knowing I'd have a friend to chat with as I ventured into the book exhibits. I wish Jim the best of retirements!

JOE D. SEGER
Mississippi State University

IT IS A PRIVILEGE TO BE A CONTRIBUTOR TO THIS BOOK OF REFLEC-
tions honoring the life work of Jim and Merna Eisenbraun. In the
mid-1970s as some of us were launching careers in field archaeology
and biblical studies, Jim's training as a graduate student in Near Eastern Studies at the University of Michigan, prompted him to take a left
turn (actually as it turned out "THE RIGHT turn") into the field of
academic publication. He was, I believe, inspired and mentored by Professor David Noel Freedman, who was then intimately involved in the
publication efforts for the American Schools of Oriental Research, and
through the years Eisenbrauns has continued to support ASOR's publications with production work.

Flash forward a few decades. By the 1990s Eisenbrauns Inc. had
become a household name among scholars working in the disciplines
of ancient Near Eastern studies. Along with that, Jim and Merna were
well-known friendly faces at the book fairs of regional, national, and
international professional meetings.

In these years my own work as director of excavations in Israel
at Gezer for Hebrew Union College, and at Tell Halif for the Lahav
Research Project had continued apace. So, as the time arrived to plan
for the publication of final reports on these endeavors, contacting Jim
was a no-brainer.

While Jim was not trained as a field archaeologist, he had clearly
learned to indulge the peculiarities of our reporting needs and styles,
actively lending his personal attentions to help his staff accommodate
our whims. Having worked with him now for two plus decades on the
production and publication of ten different archaeological report volumes. I view him as an adopted member of our research cadre. His
collaboration and mentoring are sincerely valued as a cherished gift.

And beyond all this, Eisenbrauns' service to scholarship in the
history, religion, and languages of the ancient Near Eastern world
have much more widely flourished, producing vital resources for
understanding in the Humanities. Now as an imprint of Penn State

University Press, Eisenbrauns' mission will endure. Jim and Merna can be rightly proud of their life's work, and well deserve our warmest thanks for the many contributions to scholarship they have promoted and enabled.

DIANE M. SHARON
Skirball Academy at the Streicker Center of Temple Emanuel

IN THE SPRING OF 1995 I HAD COMPLETED MY DISSERTATION FOR A Ph.D. at JTS in Hebrew Bible and Ancient Near Eastern Languages. Teachers and mentors had suggested revising it for publication, and I sent a book proposal to Jim Eisenbraun. Eisenbrauns had been the publisher of so many of the resources I used as a graduate student at JTS and in the courses I took in ancient Near Eastern languages at Penn and Yale that I felt my work was a good fit for the company and that my approach would be appreciated. In the fall of 1995 I received a letter from Jim Eisenbraun asking to see the MS, which I sent. Some months later I received a detailed response from him, accepting the project for publication. Jim suggested specific ways to sharpen the focus and also suggesting areas to expand. Characteristically, he asked me to concentrate on answering the "so what?" question for each section, and suggested ways to appeal to even the academic reader with specific examples and broadened discussion. His insightful suggestions were extremely valuable in helping this newly-minted scholar to transition from student to professional.

My personal experience of Jim's intelligence, sound instincts, and generosity are only a reflection in miniature of Jim's enormous contribution to the fields of ancient Near Eastern studies, archaeology, and biblical scholarship. Eisenbrauns' back-list is an invaluable and unique resource for scholarship in ancient literature and culture, Hebrew Bible, archaeology, linguistics, and comparative studies. Jim's concern with the preservation and comprehension of ancient civilizations, and his commitment to studies in the humanities, have been an important beacon among an increasing academic focus upon the sciences. His legacy is profound and broad, and resonates beyond the bounds of a single person or institution. It touches the future of every field he championed.

JEAN LOUIS SKA
Pontifical Biblical Institute

A PAIR OF SPECTACLES, A MANE OF CURLY HAIR ALWAYS IN MOVEMENT, a large smile, all of that sitting in many conferences of the Society of Biblical Literature behind a computer, or towering on top of a large and skinny body among piles of books, always ready to find a volume on a shelve or to rummage in files and catalogues, this is the image I keep in mind when evoking our dear Jim. I am very grateful to him for having published the English translation of my *Introduction to Reading the Pentateuch* and for all the necessary help he offered to achieve this task. Dear Jim, you are now part of the memories I cherish and that will leap to my mind every time I see the badge SBL appear on my screen. Your jovial silhouette is inseparable from the simple idea of a biblical congress. For all that I have only one word, sung however with the best music of gratitude, "thank you."

JOHN R. SPENCER
John Carroll University

I AM PLEASED AND HONORED TO OFFER THE FOLLOWING COMMENTS IN tribute to Jim Eisenbraun. I have known and worked with Jim and his staff at Eisenbrauns for over twenty-five years. In all of that time he has been nothing but helpful and considerate.

First of all I want to applaud Jim and his publishing house for their willingness to publish the results of archaeological expeditions even though we all know there will never be a large demand for such volumes. Of course, this is a service to all of the various expeditions, but more importantly it is a significant contribution to the scholarly world. Without Jim there would likely be far fewer volumes to consult and the future generations of archaeologists and scholars would be deprived of numerous resources.

More specifically, for many years Eisenbrauns has been the publisher of the volumes from the Tell el-Hesi Joint Archaeological Expedition. I worked with him as the treasurer of the Hesi Expedition and as an editor for one of its early volumes. Whether a massive volume on the Persian period finds, with numerous sometimes complicated "pull outs," and a "slip-cover," or a more straightforward volume on the Muslim cemetery, Jim and his staff have been a constant source of support and assistance for Hesi. And in all of this he has maintained a relationship with ASOR as our joint publisher of the volumes under the series category of ASOR Excavation Reports

I have also worked with Jim and his staff as lead editor on the publication of a recent Festschrift for Sy Gitin. This type of publication is another area that Jim has been willing to enter, even knowing its limited appeal. A look at the Eisenbrauns catalogue reveals the number of such honorary and memorial volumes that he has published. These ventures have allowed the celebration of numerous scholars. It has also made it possible for both seasoned and newly-minted scholars to get their work into print. It has allowed articles that are important and obscure, long and short, rich and thin, to see the daylight and thus to enhance again the scholarly world. And in the case of the Gitin volume he also published both Israeli and Palestinian scholars. Many thanks and much recognition for his continued support of this type of publication goes to Jim

Mentioning Jim's staff is an important part of the lauding Jim. He set the tone and established the high standards that permeated his staff. This resulted in quality publications. I know that some get impatient with the timing of publications, but the number of volumes published and the quality of the work easily make up for it. My applause to Jim and his staff

Finally, I want to say something about the person. Jim has consistently been friendly and approachable. He always has time for conversation and interaction with people. He is able to accommodate unusual requests, and he makes the editors and writers of volumes his first priority. It has been a real pleasure to work with Jim, his wife Merna, and his staff at Eisenbrauns. Thank you for all that you have done.

BRENT A. STRAWN
Duke University

IT WAS *the ibex* THAT GOT ME—THAT STYLIZED IBEX WHICH SERVED AS the Eisenbrauns logo. I only learned later, when I began studying iconography, that it was adopted from a Mesopotamian cylinder seal. (I only learned recently that the ibex was evidently named, in house, as "Rex the Ibex.") I suspect I'm not the only person who was first sucked in by that beautiful ibex with its head curving back over its body, oddly disproportionate—almost pictographic like early cuneiform—further adding to the mysteries of the ancient Near East that I had become enamored with as a graduate student and that was Eisenbrauns bread and butter stock-in-trade.

Yes, it was the ibex ... *and the binding*: the printed case binding that Eisenbrauns specialized in early on and which they published in almost exclusively by the time I became an addicted customer. Eisenbrauns books were made to last and also made to look good—starting with that ibex on the spine.

The ibex, the binding ... *and the high quality content*. Eisenbrauns books were the best. The most technical publications were frequently, often exclusively, found with Eisenbrauns; that meant that the most important publications were often found solely there. And if these publications weren't first produced by Eisenbrauns, then they were at least distributed in North America by Eisenbrauns. This does not yet mention how many graduate student libraries (and professors' libraries as well!) benefited from the used book trade that Eisenbrauns dealt in on the side for many years. But back to original publications: who else published Festschriften with abandon like Jim Eisenbraun? There was no limit to their number, or so it seemed. It also seemed these books had no limits in size and girth. They grew thicker and thicker—chocked full of the most amazing essays and devoted to the most deserving of scholars. To this day, one of my favorite corners of my library are the shelves filled with nothing but Eisenbrauns Festschriften. What a gift to the honorees of these volumes! But also what a gift to the editors of and contributors to these books (I know, firsthand, as a coeditor of an Eisenbrauns Festschrift) as well as to the guild—these volumes will be mined for decades to come as fecund fields providing soil for new research, new ideas, or, perhaps better, they are fields hiding countless treasures of great price. And don't even get me started on the Eisen-products: the coffee mugs were always my favorite.

So, the ibex, the beautiful binding, the fantastic content, the distribution, the Eisen-swag...*and the people.* I say "people," plural, because Jim would be the first to say it wasn't just him; Merna alone and above all deserves mention and pride of place! But since this is a tribute to Jim, I'll focus on him—even if he is representative of many others (and he is). I first wrote to Jim as a Master's student: I was taking Ugaritic and Akkadian at the same institution that Doug Miller and Mark Shipp attended. Miller and Shipp composed *An Akkadian Handbook* during their student days and that piece was published by Jim in 1996 (second edition: 2014). Inspired by them and their publishing success—and the ibex no doubt—I got a similar idea and so wrote Jim a letter about it (that is how it was done back in the LBA). I had no business proposing the idea at my stage of career but what do you know but Jim actually wrote back! Not only that, he liked the idea and encouraged it ... and me. He wanted to hear and see more and, eventually, years later, the book—in a much different and improved iteration, with some coauthors—was placed under contract (we hope it will appear soon). But what struck me as equally, if not more, amazing than Jim's interest in an idea from a nobody graduate student way back when was how he treated me at that time: with such kindness and professionalism, as if I were an established scholar in the field, which I most certainly was not. Several years later, I found myself on the opposite end of an email from Jim, inviting me, a recent PhD graduate in my first tenure-track job, to dinner during an ASOR meeting. I'm quite confident that Jim could've had dinner with anyone at that meeting; in fact, I wasn't even attending ASOR that year! But there Jim was, inviting me to a delicious Italian feast in downtown Atlanta and treating me, again, as if I was someone noteworthy when, again, I most certainly was not.

I am acutely aware, then, that I owe a great deal to Jim. Sure there's that intoxicating ibex, the attractive printed case binding, the great

196 "He Inscribed upon a Stone": Celebrating the Work of Jim Eisenbraun

books in terms of print, design, and content (a trifecta), but it's been Jim's kindness and friendship that have left the deepest impression on me—far beyond his support for certain projects and publication of certain works of mine. Here is a gentle giant, with hair Sargon would surely have been jealous of and with the stamina of Gilgamesh when it came to editorial *Sitzfleisch*. And yet, despite knowing everybody and pretty much everything (or so it seemed to me), he acted like he had all the time in the world if you had the good fortune of catching him in the bookstalls at SBL, or happened to drop him an email about an idea or inquiry. His interest and support helped me become the scholar I am today, in part because he acted as if I was that kind of scholar long before I was.

Here is a last vignette as further proof of Jim's personal, even life-giving touch: I was shocked one Sunday morning when I opened my email before heading off to church in Savannah, Georgia, that Jim had seen a Facebook post from my family the day before. He and Merna happened to be in the area, vacationing and bird-watching (these two go hand-in-hand for the Eisenbrauns), but, having seen the post, they now planned on coming to the Methodist church where I was guest preaching. And so it was that there they were, after the first service, once again sharing their time, their generosity, their goodness and light with me, my family, and several other good souls in the foyer that morning. Of course, in retrospect, I shouldn't have been shocked at all: that's the kind of people they are, that's the kind of person Jim is. And that, beyond all else (but in truth underneath it all, supporting it all), is what has left an indelible and to my mind irreplaceable mark on our field.

Thank you, Jim. You will be sorely missed, but I wish you and Merna much joy in retirement coupled with lots and lots of birds … and maybe an ibex or two!

JOHN STRONG
Missouri State University

ONCE UPON A TIME, THE MAYOR OF A SMALL TOWN—ACTUALLY IT WAS more of a village than a town, if that, even—stepped before a small gathering of its citizens. "We need to make our mark in this world!" he proclaimed boldly, confidently. "We need to let the world know that we are here, and we're important, and that the world just wouldn't be the same without us!" Everyone clapped, though tepidly, for they were doubtful. You see, this 'town' was located off a secondary highway, in the non-descript middle of a midwestern state, which many folks referred to derisively as 'fly-over' country. All the villagers knew this, and that, despite the aspirations and good intentions of their mayor, their little town was the fly-over-ist of all fly-over towns in their fly-over land. So, the citizens of this small burg, always polite (*of course!*), remained dubious. "I know we can do this," the mayor implored. "I know we have a contribution to make to this world that will place our name before thousands of eyes, millions even!" He was getting pretty worked up and becoming just a little bit exasperated at the less-than-enthusiastic response from his fellow citizens.

Then, a tall man, bearded, with long curly hair, sitting in the back of the room raised his hand. "I have an idea." All heads turned to see what this gentleman might have to say. "How about academic publishing in the areas of ancient Near Eastern studies, archaeology, and biblical studies?"

The room went silent. And the next year, a new mayor was voted into office.

Thank you, Jim, for your service to our disciplines. You have placed quality books on the shelves of my office. Your publications have filled my head and my lectures and my writings with visions of the ancient world. And you have even set a mug with an Akkadian hymn to beer-making in my kitchen cabinet.

I am certain, too, that the citizens of Winona Lake, Indiana—whether they know it or not—appreciate you placing the name of their town in the footnotes and bibliographies that are now read by millions world-wide.

For all your many contributions, Jim, thank you. The world of scholarship has been changed for the better because of them.

SAANA SVÄRD
University of Helsinki

THE VERY FIRST SCHOLARLY ARTICLE THAT I SUBMITTED WAS FOR A
book published by Eisenbrauns (*Sacred Marriages: The Divine-Human
Sexual Metaphor from Sumer to Early Christianity*, eds. Nissinen and
Uro, 2008). This is naturally an important and nerve-wracking state in
a scholar's career, and I distinctly remember how much care they took
with my article and how politely and clearly they suggested changes to
the text. This first impression was reinforced when I wrote for one of
the Rencontre proceedings (*Organization, Representation, and Symbols
of Power in the Ancient Near East: Proceedings of the 54th Rencontre
Assyriologique Internationale at Würzburg 20–25 July 2008*, ed. Wilhelm, 2012). Additionally, I worked with Jim regarding some issues
related to images in my monograph *Women and Power in Neo-Assyrian
Palaces*. Although it was published in 2015 by *The Neo-Assyrian Text
Corpus Project*, it was printed and distributed by Eisenbrauns.

    All these positive engagements made it very easy my colleague
Agnès Garcia-Ventura and I to embrace the possibility of publishing
our edited volume with Eisenbrauns (Saana Svärd & Agnès Garcia-
Ventura: *Studying Gender in the Ancient Near East*, 2018). While the
earlier positive engagements that I had had with my articles were
merely a slight brush with Jim and his staff, the editing process of our
volume was a full introduction to what I'd like to call "the Eisenbrauns
experience." Most people who have edited a collection of scientific
articles know that even in a best-case scenario there are various twists
and turns, frustrations and triumphs, before the book itself reaches the
bookshelves. Throughout that journey (2013–2018) Jim was a steadfast support to us, giving counsel when needed and answering emails
and questions promptly, efficiently, and above all kindly. I have no idea
how he managed this, considering how many different projects they
had going on at the same time, but it was very much appreciated by us.
I am delighted that this project has given me a chance to convey my
thanks to Jim.

KUMIKO TAKEUCHI
Global Scholars

THE NAME EISENBRAUNS BECAME FAMILIAR TO ME SHORTLY AFTER I started my postgraduate study in the Divinity Faculty of the University of Cambridge in the UK in 2010. I found many books by the publisher Eisenbrauns on the shelves of Tyndale House Residential Library where I also lived during the first year of my study. Soon I also found it quite important for researchers in the theology and biblical disciplines which publisher releases their first major work, for example, a PhD dissertation. My first book based on my second PhD work was just published and released this month. Without exception everyone asked me, "By whom?" or "Which publisher?" when I announced this feat, and everyone approvingly responded, "Good!" when I mentioned the name "Eisenbrauns." Biblical scholars favorably speak of the publisher "Eisenbrauns."

I was delighted that my PhD dissertation was accepted for publication by Eisenbrauns as part of the BBR Supplement Series. As I live in Indiana, I imagined that I could even visit and see how my book would actually be made by the publisher at Winona Lake, which is only about two-hour drive from where I live. Unfortunately for me, I found that Eisenbrauns was merging with Penn State University Press (PSUP) before I met Jim Eisenbraun in person. Jim was kind and unassuming, and even extended his invitation to visit Winona Lake as he still maintained some connection to Indiana.

When I heard about the merger, I immediately felt it would be the PSUP's gain. I returned to Tyndale House this summer and, out of curiosity, checked how many books by Eisenbrauns or the PSUP were held in the library. My search could find only five hits for the PSUP as compared to over 500 hits for Eisenbrauns. I am certain that Jim will be, and is most likely already, a great asset to the PSUP for its expansion into the academic biblical scholarship field. I wish him well and his enduring success for the new Eisenbraun-PSUP publishing endeavor.

RON E. TAPPY
Pittsburgh Theological Seminary

JIM, IT IS A PRIVILEGE TO HONOR YOU FOR YOUR LONG, DISTINGUISHED career in the publication of an extraordinary array of major works related to biblical studies, archaeology, ancient Near Eastern history, paleography and epigraphy, and so many more areas and disciplines. To accomplish anything close to what you have achieved, one must truly be a person for all seasons. Between 2001 and 2017, and especially around 2006 to 2008, I had the privilege of publishing half a dozen works through your publishing house. When the author's copies of the first one—a very long book on the archaeology of Israelite Samaria—appeared on my doorstep, I remember a feeling of complete satisfaction when I saw the design, layout, and overall appearance of the book. It was exactly what I had hoped for. And that experience set the tone for the high degree of trust I had in you as we continued to work together over the years.

I have benefited greatly not only from the impressive quality of work you have so consistently produced, but also from the constant interest in my work and steady counsel you shared with me from project to project. I can recall one day emailing some specific questions to you regarding one of the manuscripts I had recently submitted. You could easily have emailed a reply to me, but instead you picked up the phone and called. We had a lengthy conversation that eventually strayed a bit from my original questions to the utility of this or that punctuation mark, matters of word choice and semantics, general issues attending the publication process, and more. The exchange was very informative . . . and delightful. Obviously, the designers and copy editors who worked for you could have given me the basic facts pertaining to my initial questions, but the personal interest you showed in my work left a lasting impression. So it has been not only the efficient, successful business model you established and oversaw in Eisenbrauns of Winona Lake, Indiana, that has over the years placed so many scholars in diverse fields in your debt—it has also been your personal touch and winsome manner. Indeed, without the latter the former may not have become the success that it was. Each facet of your story (your business savvy and personal manner) would require of most people extraordinary commitment and hard work. You have surely invested commitment, long hours, and hard work in the business side of your career. But the other side, the personal concern and rapport you have extended to your authors, seems to those of us who have published with you to have come so easily, so naturally. They are part and parcel of who you are. So please accept my deepest appreciation and gratitude as well as my warmest wishes for continued success in all you do.

JEFFREY H. TIGAY
University of Pennsylvania

JIM'S CAREER AS A PUBLISHER SPANS FOUR DECADES AND IN THAT TIME
Eisenbrauns has become one of the world's most indispensable publishers and distributors of important scholarly books in biblical and
ancient Near Eastern studies and the archaeology of Israel. Eisenbrauns' hallmarks are high standards and meticulous editing reflective
of Jim's scholarship, elegant design, reasonable prices and, for authors
and especially for editors, the true pleasure of working with Jim and the
Eisenbrauns staff. Many thanks to you, Jim. I am very happy that you
and Penn State University Press have provided for Eisenbrauns' future,
and I hope that you will remain closely involved for a long time.

EMANUEL TOV
Hebrew University

JIM IS AND ALWAYS HAS BEEN A SPECIAL TYPE OF PUBLISHER. HE'S A publisher who understands what you are talking about. It's easy for him to talk with scholars, since he's a scholar himself. He can probably understand most of the books he publishes and can read most of the scripts featuring in his books.

Jim published one book I authored, one book I edited, and eight volumes in which I have papers. So I know him quite well because he's involved in many aspects of the work.

Above all I was struck by his fairness in matters of calculating the cost of books that he published and in setting their prices. When Michael Fishbane and I edited the Talmon Festschrift in the 1990s he was modest with his request for a convention for a bilingual book. At that time some five such Festschriften were published by Eisenbrauns for Israeli colleagues. Yes, Jim has a very good connection with Israeli colleagues and Israeli publishers whose work he represented in the USA and the rest of the world.

Jim and his wife Merna have rendered an important service to scholarship, and I wish them many additional years of continued health.

RONALD L. TROXEL
University of Wisconsin-Madison

BY THE TIME I BEGAN GRADUATE CLASSES IN THE FALL OF 1982, EISEN-
brauns publishing was the go-to source for publications in ancient
Near East and Hebrew Bible. Its reputation for publishing highly specialized research, its standard of editing, and the quality of its fonts,
paper, covers, and bindings already distinguished their products.
My first publication with Eisenbrauns was a Festschrift edited with
two onetime classmates, Dennis Magary and Kelvin Friebel, that honored our Doktorvater, Michael V. Fox (*Seeking out the Wisdom of the
Ancients*, 2005). Although we were unable to secure subvention, Jim
agreed to publish the book because, as he rightly said, Michael merited
a Festschrift. We were fortunate to have punctual contributors, and I
found working with Jim and his editors a smooth process. The result
was a product that we, Michael, and readers have valued.

Eisenbrauns was my first choice for publishing *Joel: Scope, Genres,
and Meaning* (2015). When I first spoke with Jim about the project,
he suggested that it appear in a newly established series, Critical Studies in the Hebrew Bible. He touted its aim of publishing works of less
than 60,000 words, reasonably priced, and advanced quickly to press.
His use of this series to address the ethics of academic publishing (the
question of investment of both money and time in advancing scholarship) piqued my interest. I had worked under publisher constraints on
word count before, but those were calibrated to marketing rather than
the question of what a publisher owes readers. Granted, a topic like
the book of Joel lent itself to a shorter volume, but I relished the challenge because of how Jim framed the issue. As in the previous project, I
found the publishing process smooth, with Andrew Knapp, my editor,
providing excellent critiques and guidance.

One of the hallmarks of working with Eisenbrauns was direct access
to the publisher. Jim was always available and conversations with him
were amicable and thoughtful. I continue to admire the principles and
values he exhibited in publishing. He and Merna have my best wishes

for a long and enjoyable retirement, as they undertake the projects and journeys of their choosing.

DAVID TSUMURA
Japan Bible Seminary

I HAVE ALWAYS APPRECIATED JIM EISENBRAUN FOR HIS DEDICATION AS a publisher specializing in the studies of Hebrew Bible and its world of the ancient Near East. He has often generously agreed to publish not-so-popular books and to reprint some indispensable primary sources of ancient languages, otherwise unavailable to the scholars, such as Akkadian, Sumerian, Hittite as well as Northwest Semitic. These materials help us biblical scholars to place the Bible in its original context comparatively and contrastively. Any comparative study should be rooted in a detailed knowledge of both items being compared, utilizing the primary sources. For this purpose, Jim and his staff have provided indispensable tools.

My two books published by him are such comparative studies: 'I Studied Inscriptions from Before the Flood': Ancient Near Eastern, Literary, and Linguistic Approaches to Genesis 1–11, co-edited with Richard Hess, 1994, and Creation and Destruction: A Reappraisal of the Chaoskampf Theory of the Old Testament, 2005. He also published my recent article on parallelism in Advances in Biblical Hebrew Linguistics Data, Methods, and Analyses, ed. by A. Moshavi and T. Notarius, 2017.

I especially thank Jim for his warmth toward Asian scholars. He is a descendant of the Bartel family, whom God used for His glory as missionaries to China, especially during the difficult era of the Japanese invasion of China.

May God bless Jim and keep him in His good care during his retirement.

JOHN H. WALTON
Wheaton College

JIM EISENBRAUN HAS BEEN A GIFT TO THE ACADEMICS OF THE SBL, AOS, IBR, and ASOR, just to name a few or the organizations who have been well-served by his publishing house. His vision for publishing has provided accessibility to the world of the ancient Near East and Hebrew Bible that has made possible a level of scholarship that otherwise would not have been possible. In my current writing project, a day does not go by that I don't pull at least a couple of Eisenbrauns published volumes from the shelf to research an issue or solve a problem. Many publishers might have disdained these publications as too arcane or esoteric for their attention, but Jim recognized the value of having the right piece of information (however obscure) for the question at hand. I tried to count up all of the Eisenbrauns volumes on my bookshelves, but gave up in despair when I passed 100.

Much of this has been accomplished because of Jim's ability to network so congenially with scholars around the world. Every time we sat down over a meal for conversation or stood chatting at the booth, Jim was always interested in me as a person as well as in the work that I was doing.

Finally, a comment must be made about Jim's diligence as an editor. The benefit of having Jim edit your work was not just his attention to the mechanics of style and format and other matters of editorial detail. The value of having an editor who was intimately knowledgeable about the languages and literature of the ancient Near East can scarcely be overstated. He could fact-check my data from his store of knowledge, and he cared about helping find just the right way to frame my material.

Thank you, friend—the academic world would be a poorer place without your vision and hard work. My own work would have been much more difficult, and some of it impossible.

BRUCE WELLS
University of Texas at Austin

WHEN I BEGAN MY MASTER'S PROGRAM IN THE MID-1990S, I QUICKLY
became convinced that Eisenbrauns must be one of the largest and most
distinguished academic publishers in the country. The most important books in my studies nearly all came from Eisenbrauns. I couldn't
conceive of this company as anything less than a major enterprise.
Someone soon told me that Eisenbrauns was a rather small publisher
that worked only in biblical and Near Eastern studies. I was not at all
sure my informant was reliable. Shortly after that, I found myself at a
regional conference in the Chicago area, hanging around the Eisenbrauns display table. William Dever walked up and told Jim he'd really
like to speak with him later about a book idea. I was definitely more in
awe of Jim at the time than Professor Dever, given that the esteemed
archaeologist seemed to be lobbying Jim rather than vice versa. Yes, I
decided, Eisenbrauns was a big deal.

I attended another conference in 1999 where Jim talked about
Eisenbrauns as a "tiny" outfit within the world of publishing. I still
wasn't convinced. It seemed to me that, without Eisenbrauns, I and
many others wouldn't have access to most of the books that we needed.
I figured Jim was just being modest.

I now suspect that Eisenbrauns has been a huge multinational con-
glomerate all along, coveted by most of the large publishing houses,
and Jim's been fooling us this whole time. Well, perhaps it's only slightly
more accurate to say that it was a wildly successful start-up that recently
had a very amicable merger with a university press. It goes without
saying that Eisenbrauns has been indispensable as a publisher and
distributor of books that are absolutely vital to what we do. Without
Jim's passion for biblical and Near Eastern studies and his modest, little
company, I have no idea how most of us would have survived. On top
of that, it wasn't too long after he started that it became a feather in one's
cap to publish with Jim. For years now, scholars have acknowledged
Eisenbrauns as one of the best and most highly respected publishers in
the field.

When it comes to my own publishing ventures, Eisenbrauns saved the day for me on two different occasions. In 2009, I learned that my beloved advisor, Raymond Westbrook, was dying. My colleague, F. Rachel Magdalene, and I determined to put together, as quickly, as we could, a collection of his articles and essays. But who would publish a two-volume work like this? Jim immediately saw the value in the collection and, even though he knew he might not make much money from it, signed on to publish it. In a much shorter amount of time than I anticipated, we had *Law from the Tigris to the Tiber: The Writings of Raymond Westbrook*. Numerous people have told us how much they appreciate having this collection, and it would not have happened without Jim. More recently, two colleagues and I had completed a manuscript that we thought might come out with a different publisher. We ran into a variety of problems, though, and began looking for another outlet. I sought Jim's advice, and he expressed interest in the project. We had to make some revisions, but Jim's support was unwavering throughout the whole process. I love Eisenbrauns. It's my favorite publisher to buy from and the one I buy from most often. I make a beeline to their booth at SBL every year, the moment I enter the exhibit hall. I suppose that Jim deserves a break after forty-plus years of extremely hard work. I wonder how many weekends over those years he took off. Probably not very many. From now on, we may not see him around as much as we used to, and we'll miss that a great deal. But, in good biblical fashion, his name will live on.

OLA WIKANDER
Lund University

WHEN I FIRST STARTED OUT AS A YOUNG AND EAGER STUDENT OF THE ancient Near East (beginning as a happy and intense 17-year old, reading Akkadian under the tutelage of Tryggve Mettinger), *Eisenbrauns* was a name that one heard agin and again. It was mentioned as one of the self-evident, given homes of quality scholarship in the field. And the clear reason for this—was the role of Jim Eisenbraun himself. Eisenbrauns was, indeed, a *name* unto itself.

Years later, when I was to internationally publish my dissertation *Drought, Death, and the Sun in Ugarit and Ancient Israel* and later *Unburning Fame: Horses Dragons, Beings of Smoke, and Other Indo-European Motifs in Ugarit and the Hebrew Bible*, Eisenbrauns and Jim were there, and I felt the thrill of myself working with that fabled institution. Working with Jim was a joy, as he and Andrew Knapp expertly guided me through the arduous and convoluted process of creating a camera-ready copy for a book—in Microsoft Word, no less! I stumbled along, as my skills in creating the physicality of a book, with running heads and jumping page numbers, were zero. But step by step, test-PDF by test-PDF, the books took form.

As the date of publication of one of the books grew close, and I told a few friends and colleagues from other fields about the upcoming volume, one of them exclaimed something along the lines of: "Eisenbrauns! That has got to be one of the most badass names ever for a publisher!"

Indeed—and that is name of Jim Eisenbraun.

ELLEN VAN WOLDE
Radboud University Nijmegen

EVERY YEAR AT THE SBL ANNUAL MEETING I VISITED THE EISENBRAUNS booth, admiring its collection of books. I felt at home there: ancient Near East, archeology, biblical studies- all well edited and visually attractive books, and I thought "one day I will publish my monograph with them". And so I did. In 2008 I contacted Jim, met him at the Annual Meeting, we discussed my proposal. He showed an interest in the topic, asked some challenging and practical questions, and I felt encouraged to continue working. What impressed me was that there was no difficult deal making, no legal stuff (at least as far as I remember), which did not fit my image of American publishers or of an American society filled with lawyers and legal stuff.

I submitted my book, and second surprise: a wonderful cooperation started with the copyeditor of Eisenbrauns, Mrs. Beverly McCoy: the care and accuracy with which she worked was amazing. Talking about the cover, Jim immediately understood what I meant saying that I had fractals in mind. A beautiful cover, made within a week, was the result. Jim's appreciative words about the content of the book delighted me and also after the publication Jim kept in contact, thinking about promotion, sharing ideas, etc. This is what a publisher should be, what you wish for as an author and I wish thank Jim and his team wholeheartedly.

DAN ZACHARY
Eisenbrauns, Business Manager, 2012–2017

WORKING ALONGSIDE JIM ALLOWED ME TO SEE HIS DEDICATION TO, and passion for, his desire to make the world a better place by publishing works that helped others view the areas of ancient Near East, archaeology, and biblical studies more completely. He not only enhanced this but helped make his mark through his technical expertise that characterizes Eisenbrauns publications. His work enriched the lives of those he touched in these unique fields.

Though his career intersected my work life relatively briefly, I also witnessed his love of family, loyalty to friends, fascination with nature, appreciation of music, and generosity to all. In these ways, he enriched my life.

ZIONY ZEVIT
American Jewish University

I FIRST HEARD OF JIM EISENBRAUN AT AN AOS MEETING IN THE LATE 70s: "there's this grad student at Michigan who is selling books out of his trailer. He can beat most of the prices of booksellers here." Those singing his praises were students, young and not so young scholars interested in a range of topics in ancient Near Eastern topics and biblical studies of all sorts. I placed my orders and became a fan also, even a greater fan when Jim went into publishing.

The affable smile, the warm greeting by name, the firm handshake, the natural ability to "be there" when you were talking casually or talking shop while all around the book exhibit hundreds—if not thousands, at SBL meetings—were bustling by. Jim and his whole operation, employees and family, came to signal honesty, integrity, and competence.

Beyond running a successful business that beat the pants off of many publishers in pricing books that academics (and libraries) could afford, his focus was on customers from among those who proposed volumes, browsed his new offerings, and shared ideas. More than once I heard him direct people who were very specific about what they wanted to other publishers; more often I saw people smiling, happy or content at what he had said. He was there to help, when he could. I have always enjoyed Jim's company, his gregarious shyness.

I joined those who first told me about him in the 70s by co-editing volumes with Eisenbrauns to which many of them contributed and publishing some of my own work in volumes that they have edited. All told, Jim's imprint has been a major influence in biblical and ancient Near Eastern scholarship of the late twentieth and early twenty-first centuries. His true legacy, however, is his good name. It is a major imprint.

WORDS OF THANKS

JAMES A. GREENBERG
Denver Seminary

I GREATLY APPRECIATE JIM EISENBRAUN AND HIS HELP AND ENCOUR-
agement to publish my book on atonement in Leviticus. Jim provided
excellent insight and guidance for my final manuscript. The books,
journals, and resources that Jim has brought to the world of biblical
interpretation have been invaluable to my research. It has been an
honor to work with Jim and witness his dedication to develop, pro-
mote, and publish scholarly works.

MARLIES HEINZ
Albert Ludwigs-University

I WOULD LIKE TO THANK JIM EISENBRAUN FOR HIS EXCELLENT SUPPORT
of our 2007 book project: Marian Feldman and Marlies Heinz, eds.,
*Representations of Political Power: Case Histories from Times of Change
and Dissolving Order in the Ancient Near East.*

KAROLIEN VERMEULEN AND ELIZABETH HAYES
University of Antwerp and Fuller Theological Seminary

KINDNESS. IT IS A SIMPLE BUT INVALUABLE TRAIT WHEN IT COMES TO
the academic publishing business. As the biblical proverb goes, "many
are called, but few are chosen" (Matt 22:4). We were pleased to see that
Jim belongs to the latter category, gifted with a kindness that makes the
business a little friendlier and the life of authors and editors far more
enjoyable.
　　Thank you , Jim!

A. RAHEL WELLS
Andrews University

EXCELLENT SCHOLARSHIP. EXEMPLARY PUBLISHING WORK. EDITORIAL expertise. These are just a few of the things that Jim Eisenbraun has brought to biblical and theological studies over his many years of service. I am so grateful for his dedication, ministry, and vision. He will be much missed, but I am certain that his legacy will live on and inspire us all for many many years to come.

TYLER YODER
Culver Academies

JIM, YOUR TRANSPARENCY AND SAGE COUNSEL OFFERED AN EXEMplary guide as I explored the market for my first book. I am sincerely grateful for the kindness you showed me along the way, exuding care both for my work and for me as a person. Thank you for your steadfast commitment to reveal the ancient Near East to the world in the form of rigorous and responsible scholarship.

www.ingramcontent.com/pod-product-compliance
Lightning Source LLC
Chambersburg PA
CBHW041254160426

42812CB00084B/2514